papyrus

IMHOTEP'S TRANSFORMATION

BY DE GIETER.

Papyrus and Theti-Cheri fed by the Goddess of Trees.

9th CINEBOOK
The 9th Art Publisher

Original title: Papyrus – La métamorphose d'Imhotep

Original edition: © Dupuis, 1985
by De Gieter
www.dupuis.com

English translation: © 2008 Cinebook Ltd

Translator: Luke Spear
Lettering and Text layout: Imadjinn sarl
Printed in Spain by Just Colour Graphic

This edition first published in Great Britain in 2008 by
CINEBOOK Ltd
56 Beech Avenue
Canterbury, Kent
CT4 7TA
www.cinebook.com

A CIP catalogue record for this book
is available from the British Library

ISBN 978-1-905460-50-2

9th CINEBOOK
The 9th Art Publisher

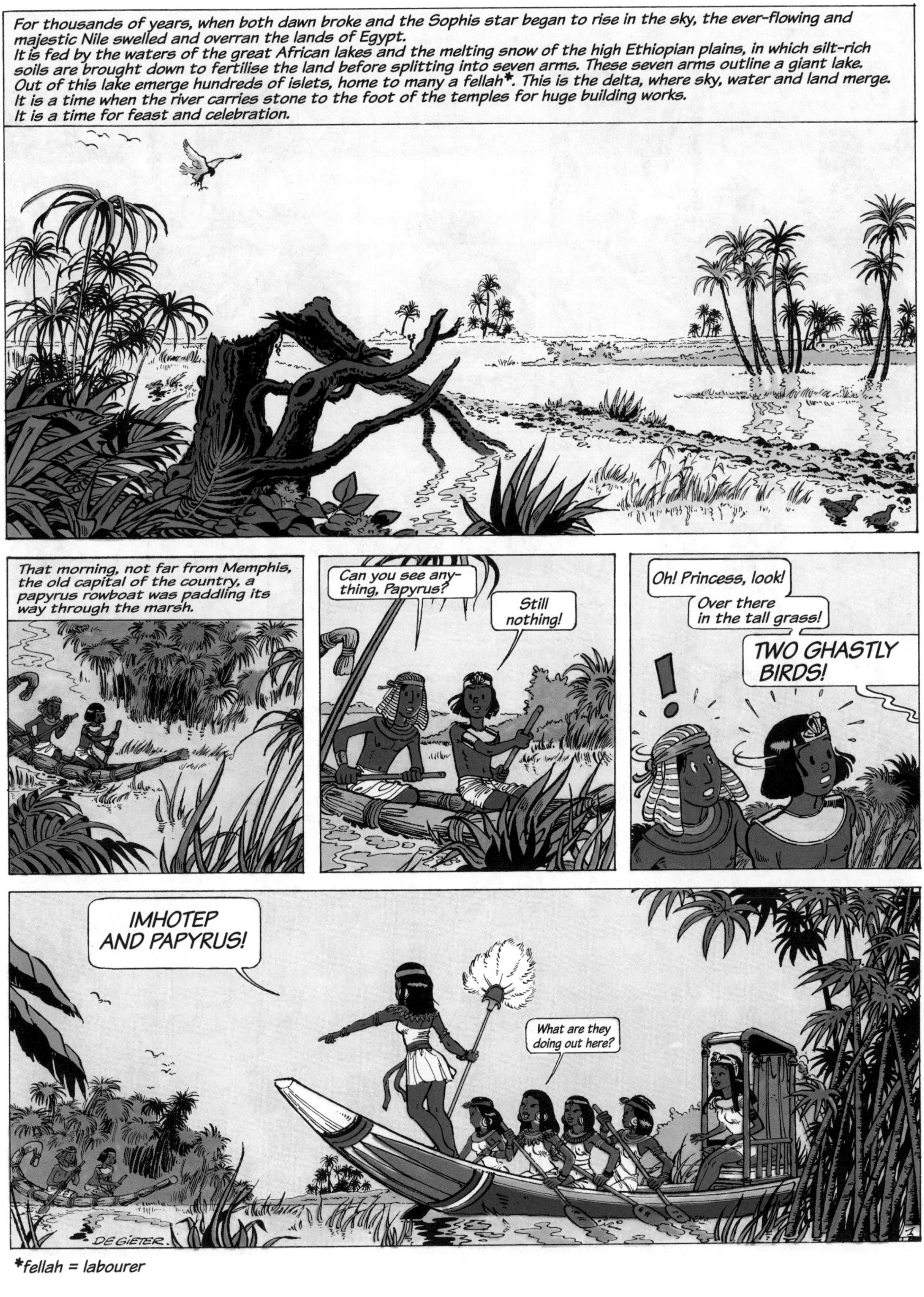
For thousands of years, when both dawn broke and the Sophis star began to rise in the sky, the ever-flowing and majestic Nile swelled and overran the lands of Egypt.
It is fed by the waters of the great African lakes and the melting snow of the high Ethiopian plains, in which silt-rich soils are brought down to fertilise the land before splitting into seven arms. These seven arms outline a giant lake.
Out of this lake emerge hundreds of islets, home to many a fellah*. This is the delta, where sky, water and land merge.
It is a time when the river carries stone to the foot of the temples for huge building works.
It is a time for feast and celebration.
That morning, not far from Memphis, the old capital of the country, a papyrus rowboat was paddling its way through the marsh.
Can you see anything, Papyrus?
Still nothing!
Oh! Princess, look!
Over there in the tall grass!
TWO GHASTLY BIRDS!
!
IMHOTEP AND PAPYRUS!
What are they doing out here?
DE GIETER

*fellah = labourer

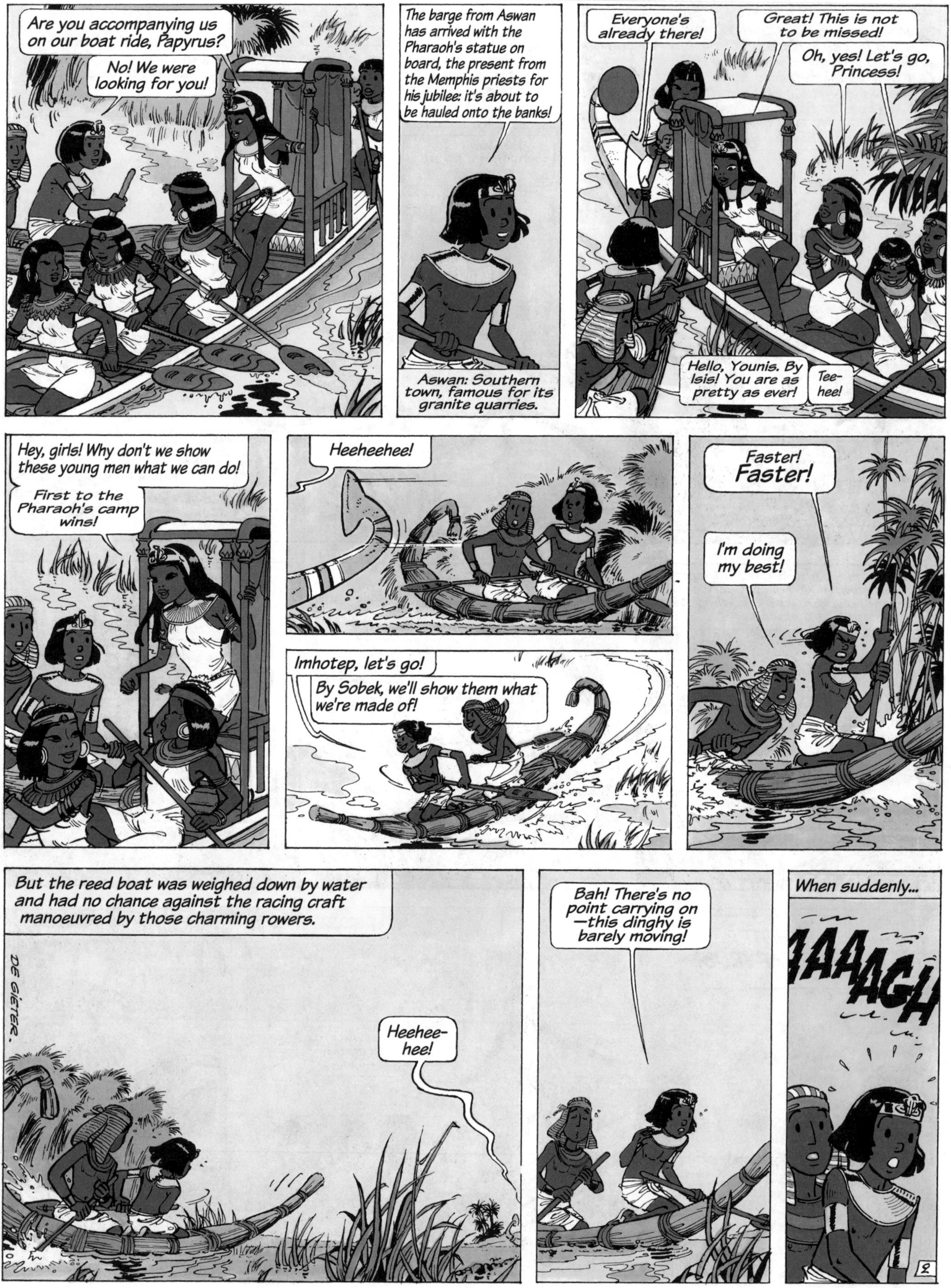
Are you accompanying us on our boat ride, Papyrus?
No! We were looking for you!
The barge from Aswan has arrived with the Pharaoh's statue on board, the present from the Memphis priests for his jubilee: it's about to be hauled onto the banks!
Aswan: Southern town, famous for its granite quarries.
Everyone's already there!
Great! This is not to be missed!
Oh, yes! Let's go, Princess!
Hello, Younis. By Isis! You are as pretty as ever!
Tee-hee!
Hey, girls! Why don't we show these young men what we can do!
First to the Pharaoh's camp wins!
Heeheehee!
Imhotep, let's go!
By Sobek, we'll show them what we're made of!
Faster! Faster!
I'm doing my best!
But the reed boat was weighed down by water and had no chance against the racing craft manoeuvred by those charming rowers.
DE GIETER.
Heehee-hee!
Bah! There's no point carrying on —this dinghy is barely moving!
When suddenly...
AAAAGH
2

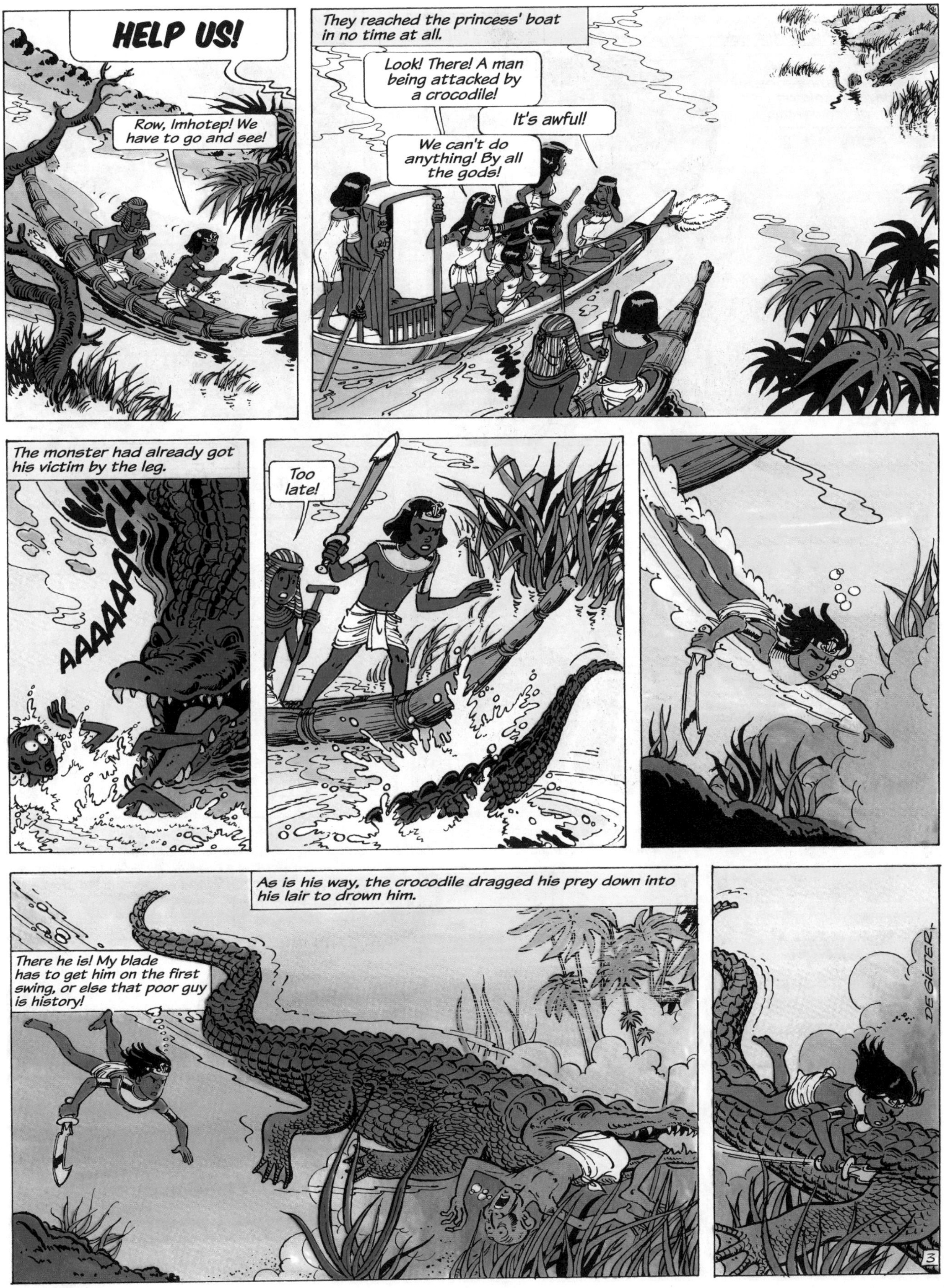
HELP US!
Row, Imhotep! We have to go and see!
They reached the princess' boat in no time at all.
Look! There! A man being attacked by a crocodile!
It's awful!
We can't do anything! By all the gods!
The monster had already got his victim by the leg.
AAAAAAGH
Too late!
As is his way, the crocodile dragged his prey down into his lair to drown him.
There he is! My blade has to get him on the first swing, or else that poor guy is history!
DE GIETER
3

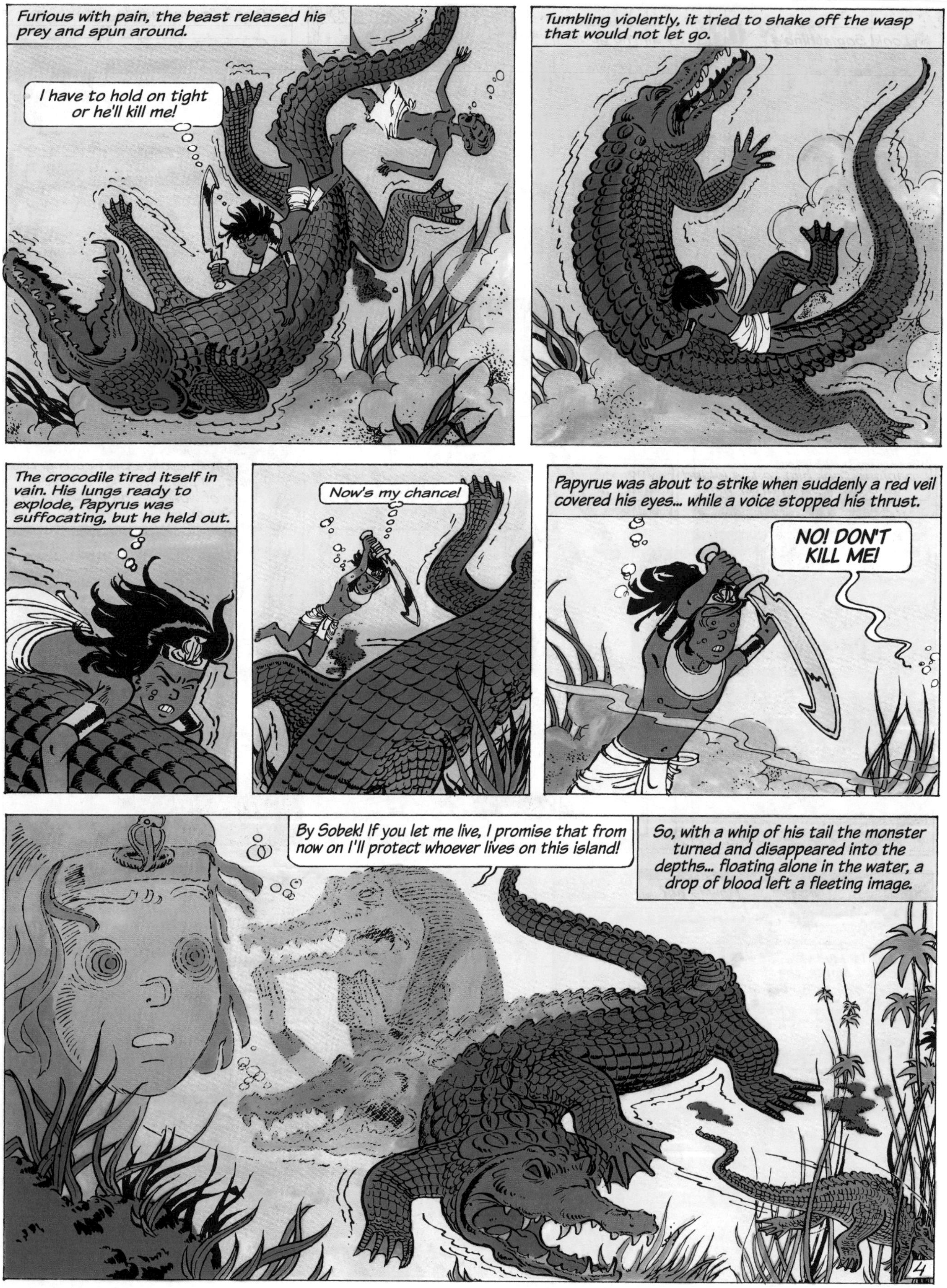
Furious with pain, the beast released his prey and spun around.
I have to hold on tight or he'll kill me!
Tumbling violently, it tried to shake off the wasp that would not let go.
The crocodile tired itself in vain. His lungs ready to explode, Papyrus was suffocating, but he held out.
Now's my chance!
Papyrus was about to strike when suddenly a red veil covered his eyes... while a voice stopped his thrust.
NO! DON'T KILL ME!
By Sobek! If you let me live, I promise that from now on I'll protect whoever lives on this island!
So, with a whip of his tail the monster turned and disappeared into the depths... floating alone in the water, a drop of blood left a fleeting image.
4

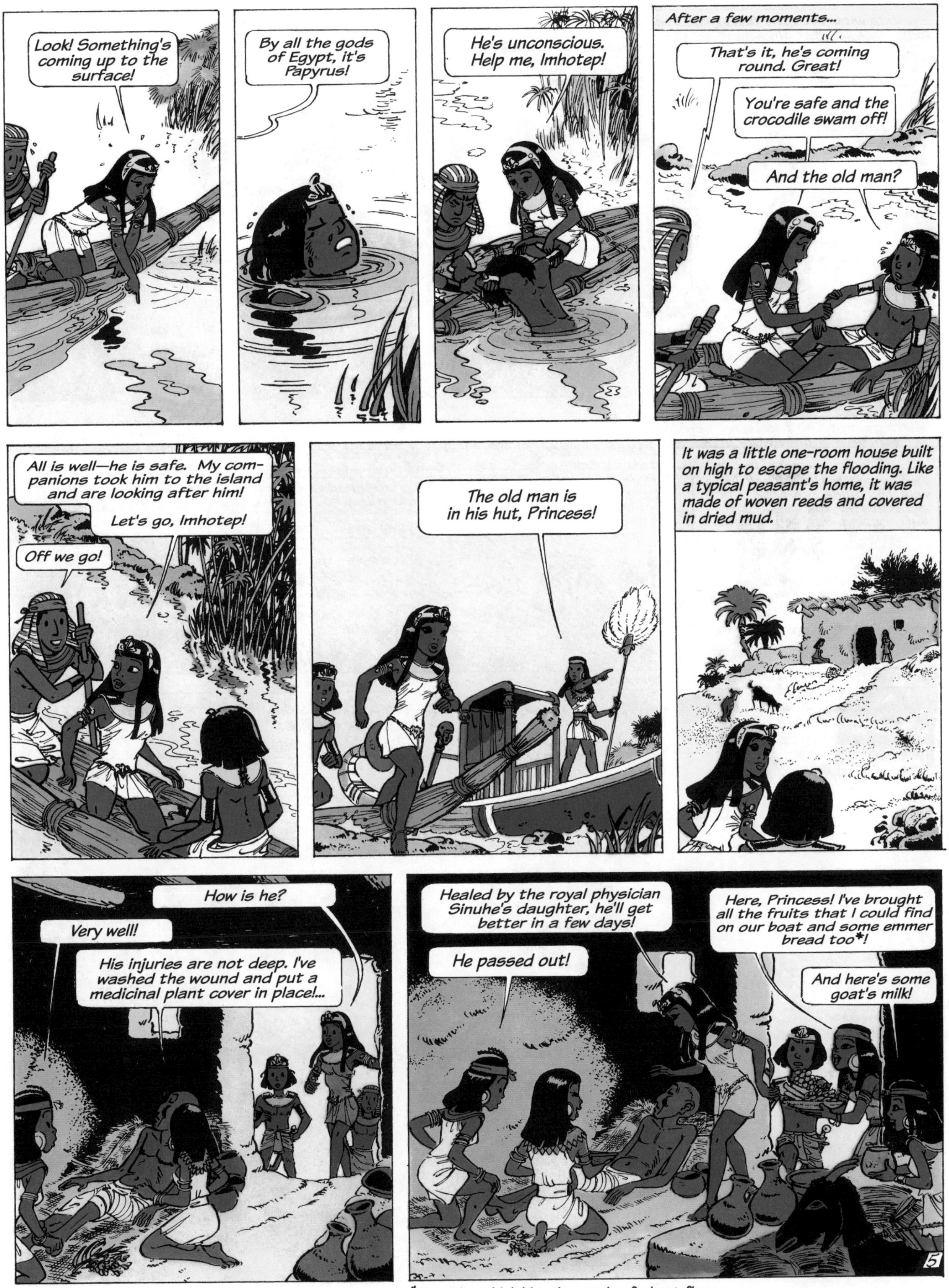
Look! Something's coming up to the surface!
By all the gods of Egypt, it's Papyrus!
He's unconscious. Help me, Imhotep!
After a few moments...
That's it, he's coming round. Great!
You're safe and the crocodile swam off!
And the old man?
All is well—he is safe. My companions took him to the island and are looking after him!
Let's go, Imhotep!
Off we go!
The old man is in his hut, Princess!
It was a little one-room house built on high to escape the flooding. Like a typical peasant's home, it was made of woven reeds and covered in dried mud.
How is he?
Very well!
His injuries are not deep. I've washed the wound and put a medicinal plant cover in place!...
Healed by the royal physician Sinuhe's daughter, he'll get better in a few days!
He passed out!
Here, Princess! I've brought all the fruits that I could find on our boat and some emmer bread too*!
And here's some goat's milk!
5

*Egyptian thick biscuits made of wheat flour.

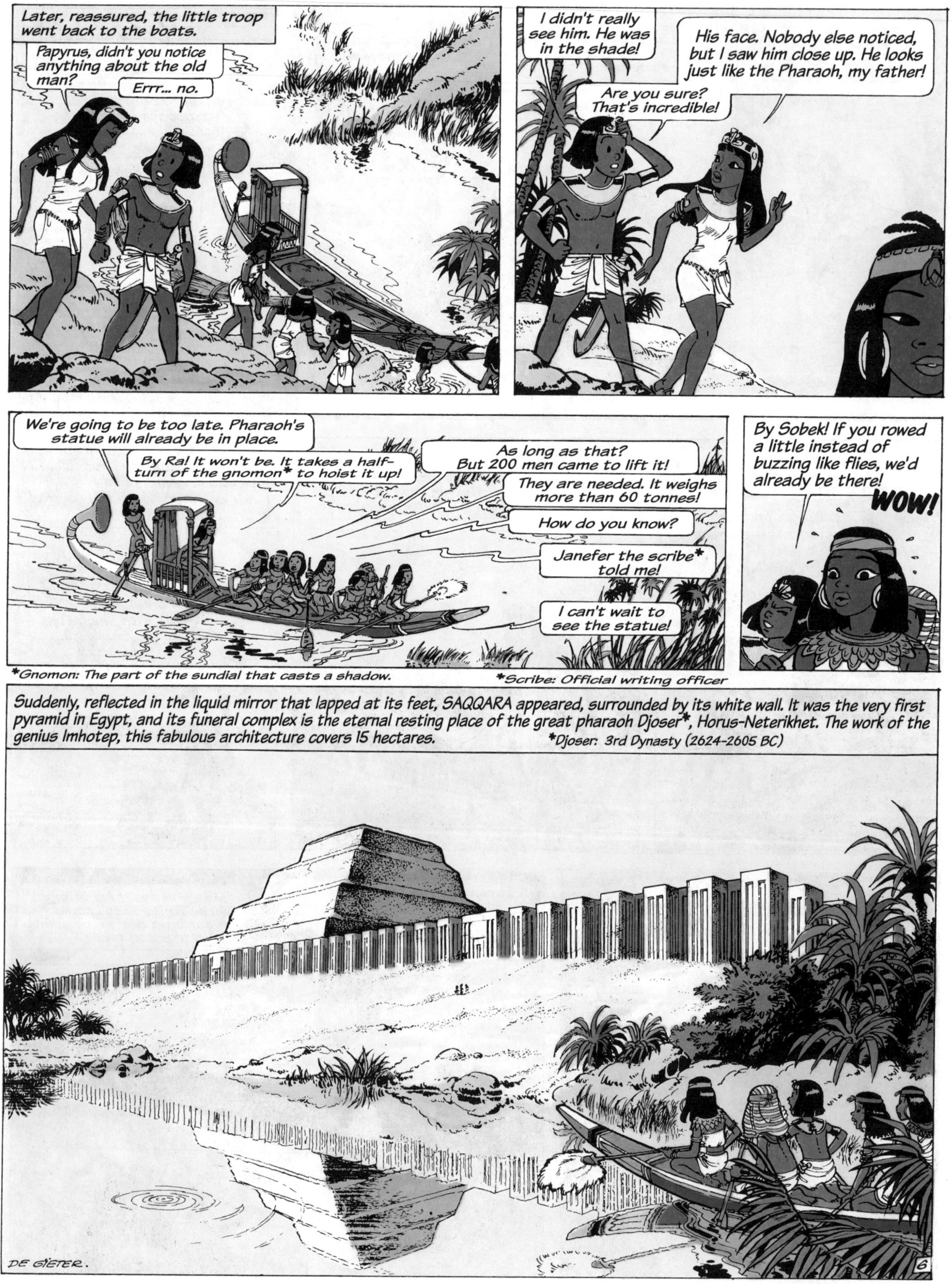
Later, reassured, the little troop went back to the boats.
Papyrus, didn't you notice anything about the old man?
Errr... no.
I didn't really see him. He was in the shade!
His face. Nobody else noticed, but I saw him close up. He looks just like the Pharaoh, my father!
Are you sure? That's incredible!
We're going to be too late. Pharaoh's statue will already be in place.
By Ra! It won't be. It takes a half-turn of the gnomon* to hoist it up!
As long as that? But 200 men came to lift it!
They are needed. It weighs more than 60 tonnes!
How do you know?
Janefer the scribe* told me!
I can't wait to see the statue!
By Sobek! If you rowed a little instead of buzzing like flies, we'd already be there!
WOW!
*Gnomon: The part of the sundial that casts a shadow.
*Scribe: Official writing officer
Suddenly, reflected in the liquid mirror that lapped at its feet, SAQQARA appeared, surrounded by its white wall. It was the very first pyramid in Egypt, and its funeral complex is the eternal resting place of the great pharaoh Djoser*, Horus-Neterikhet. The work of the genius Imhotep, this fabulous architecture covers 15 hectares.
*Djoser: 3rd Dynasty (2624-2605 BC)
DE GIETER.
6

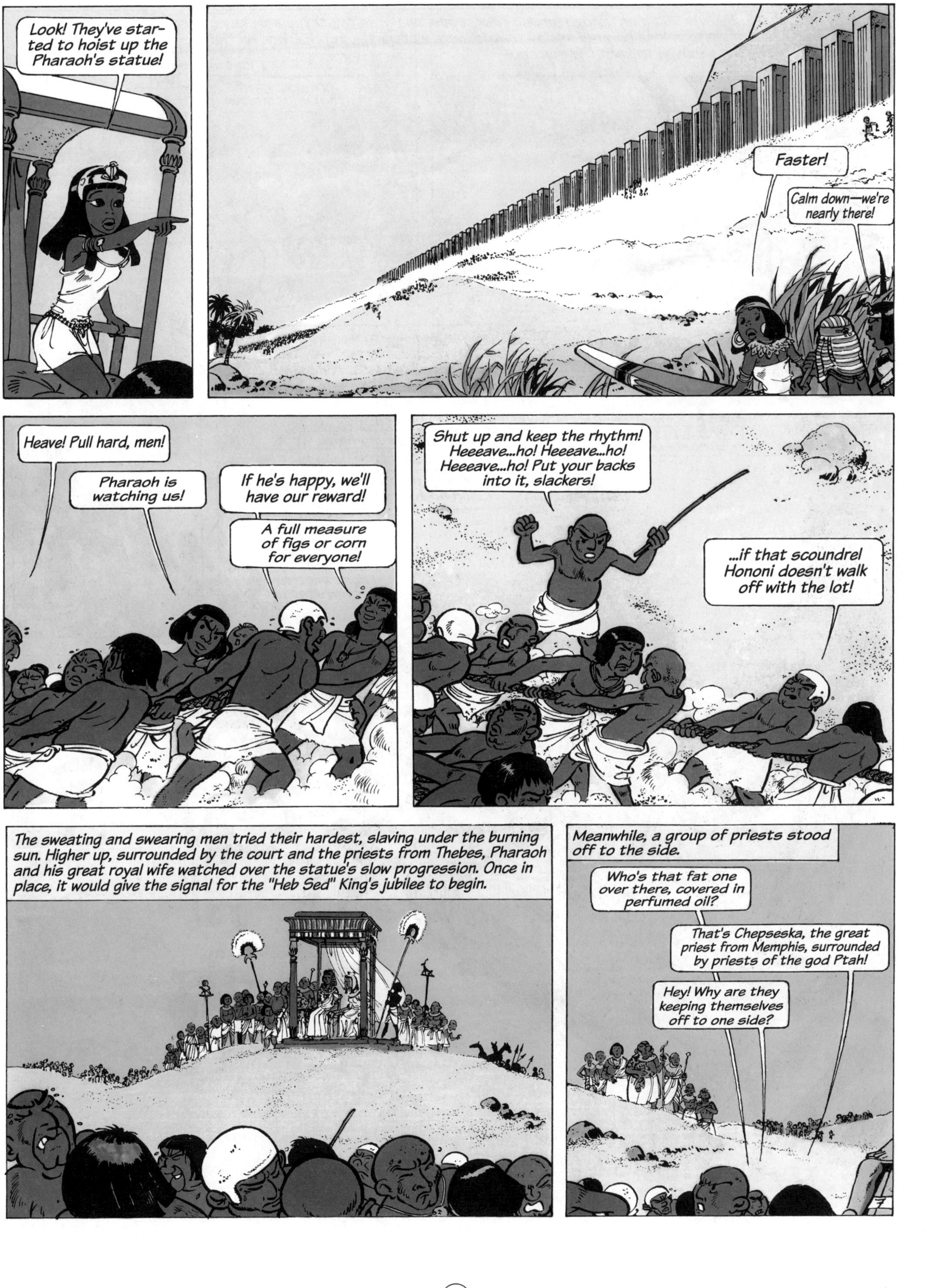
Look! They've started to hoist up the Pharaoh's statue!
Faster!
Calm down—we're nearly there!
Heave! Pull hard, men!
Pharaoh is watching us!
If he's happy, we'll have our reward!
A full measure of figs or corn for everyone!
Shut up and keep the rhythm! Heeeave...ho! Heeeave...ho! Heeeave...ho! Put your backs into it, slackers!
...if that scoundrel Hononi doesn't walk off with the lot!
The sweating and swearing men tried their hardest, slaving under the burning sun. Higher up, surrounded by the court and the priests from Thebes, Pharaoh and his great royal wife watched over the statue's slow progression. Once in place, it would give the signal for the "Heb Sed" King's jubilee to begin.
Meanwhile, a group of priests stood off to the side.
Who's that fat one over there, covered in perfumed oil?
That's Chepseska, the great priest from Memphis, surrounded by priests of the god Ptah!
Hey! Why are they keeping themselves off to one side?

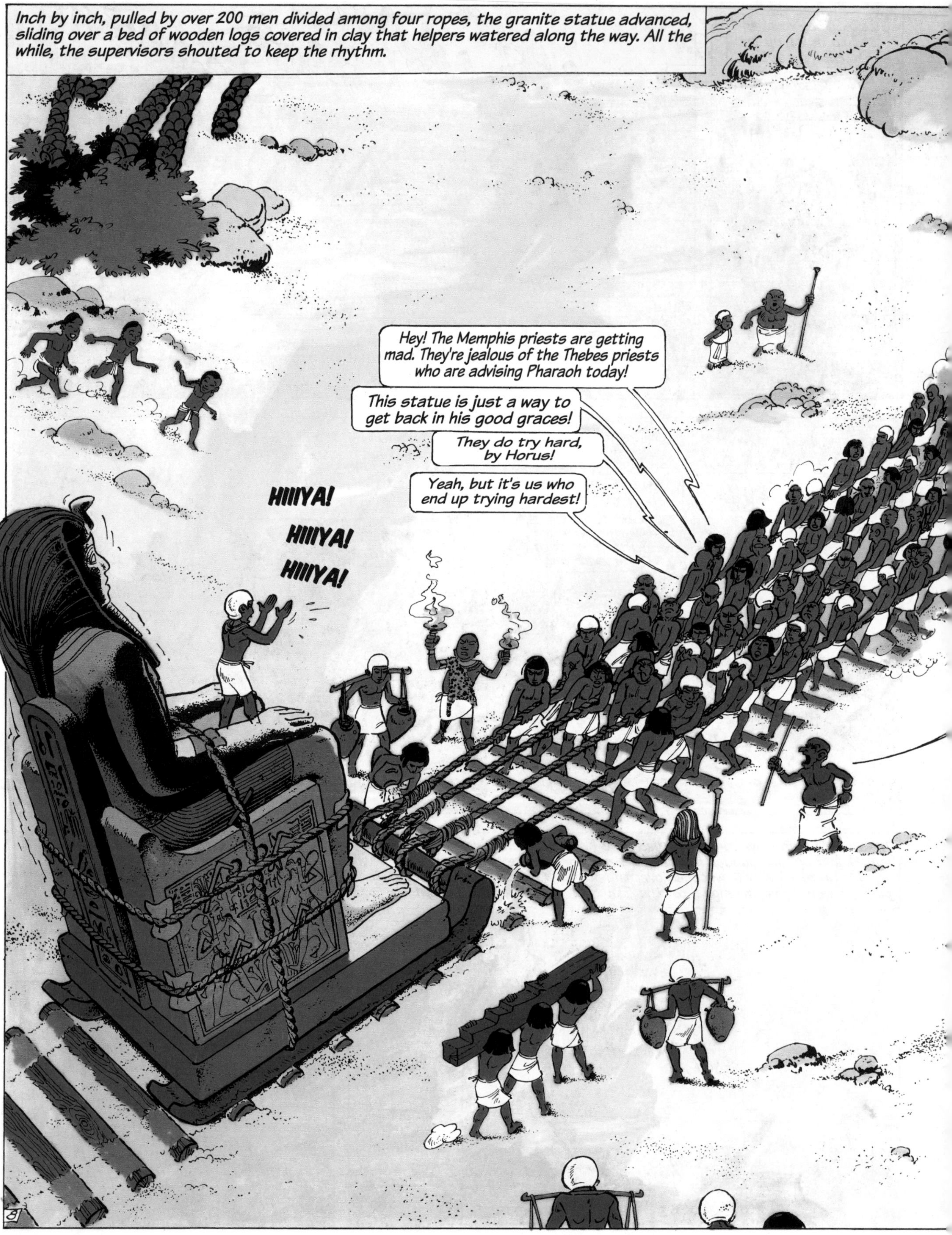
Inch by inch, pulled by over 200 men divided among four ropes, the granite statue advanced, sliding over a bed of wooden logs covered in clay that helpers watered along the way. All the while, the supervisors shouted to keep the rhythm.
Hey! The Memphis priests are getting mad. They're jealous of the Thebes priests who are advising Pharaoh today!
This statue is just a way to get back in his good graces!
They do try hard, by Horus!
Yeah, but it's us who end up trying hardest!
HIIIYA!
HIIIYA!
HIIIYA!

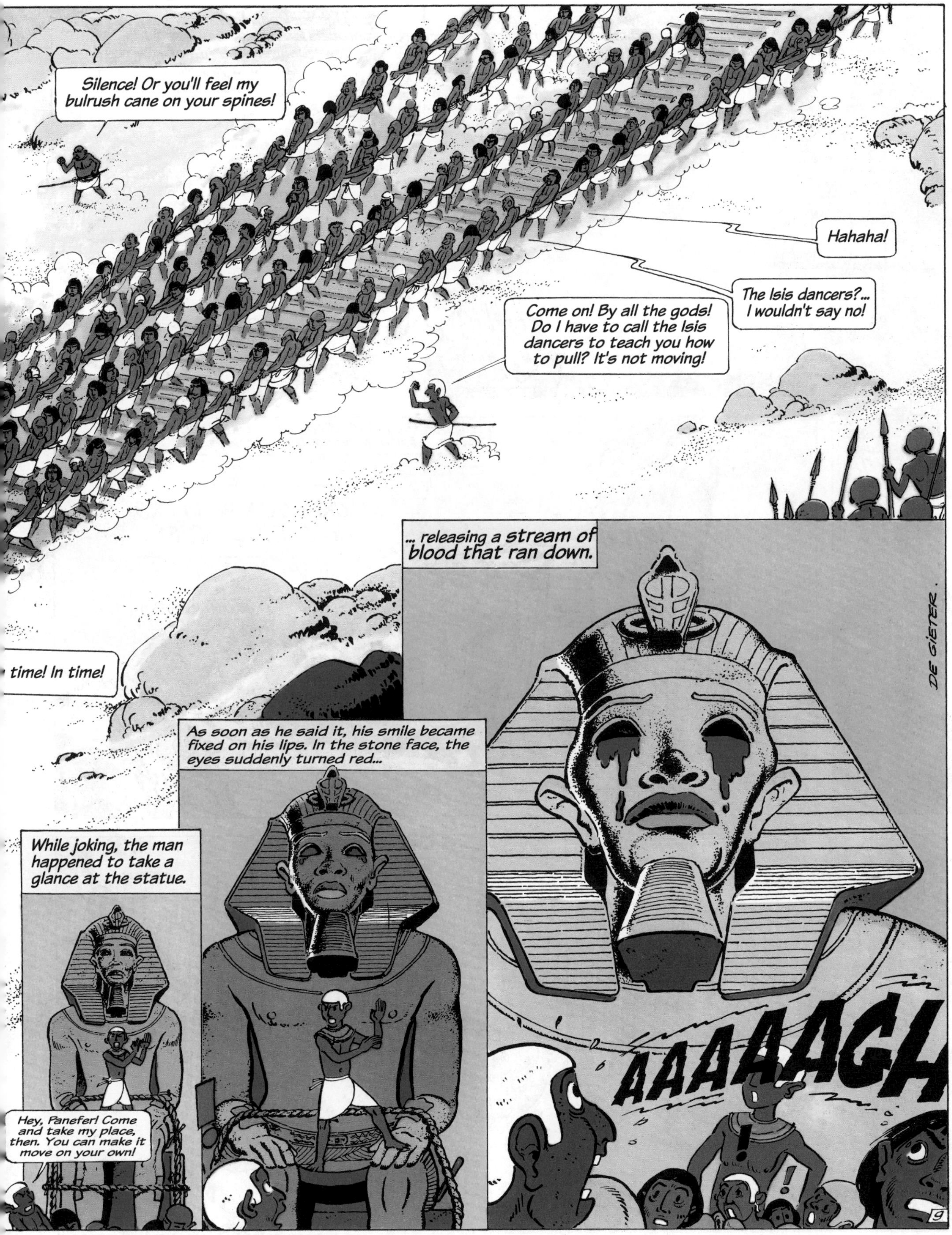
Silence! Or you'll feel my bulrush cane on your spines!
Hahaha!
The Isis dancers?... I wouldn't say no!
Come on! By all the gods! Do I have to call the Isis dancers to teach you how to pull? It's not moving!
time! In time!
While joking, the man happened to take a glance at the statue.
Hey, Panefer! Come and take my place, then. You can make it move on your own!
As soon as he said it, his smile became fixed on his lips. In the stone face, the eyes suddenly turned red...
... releasing a stream of blood that ran down.
DE GIETER
AAAAAGH
9

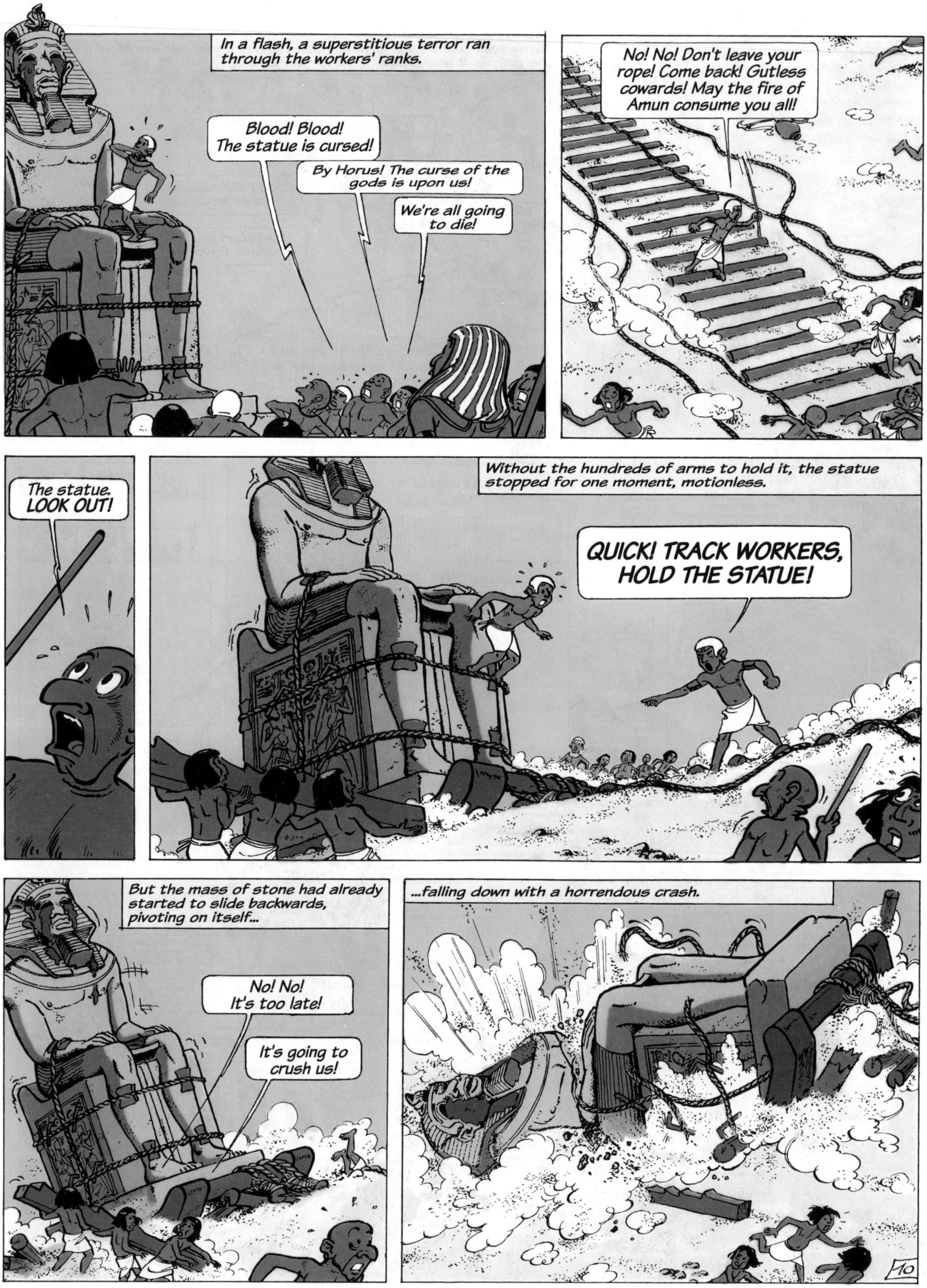
In a flash, a superstitious terror ran through the workers' ranks.
Blood! Blood! The statue is cursed!
By Horus! The curse of the gods is upon us!
We're all going to die!
No! No! Don't leave your rope! Come back! Gutless cowards! May the fire of Amun consume you all!
The statue. LOOK OUT!
Without the hundreds of arms to hold it, the statue stopped for one moment, motionless.
QUICK! TRACK WORKERS, HOLD THE STATUE!
But the mass of stone had already started to slide backwards, pivoting on itself...
No! No! It's too late!
It's going to crush us!
...falling down with a horrendous crash.
10

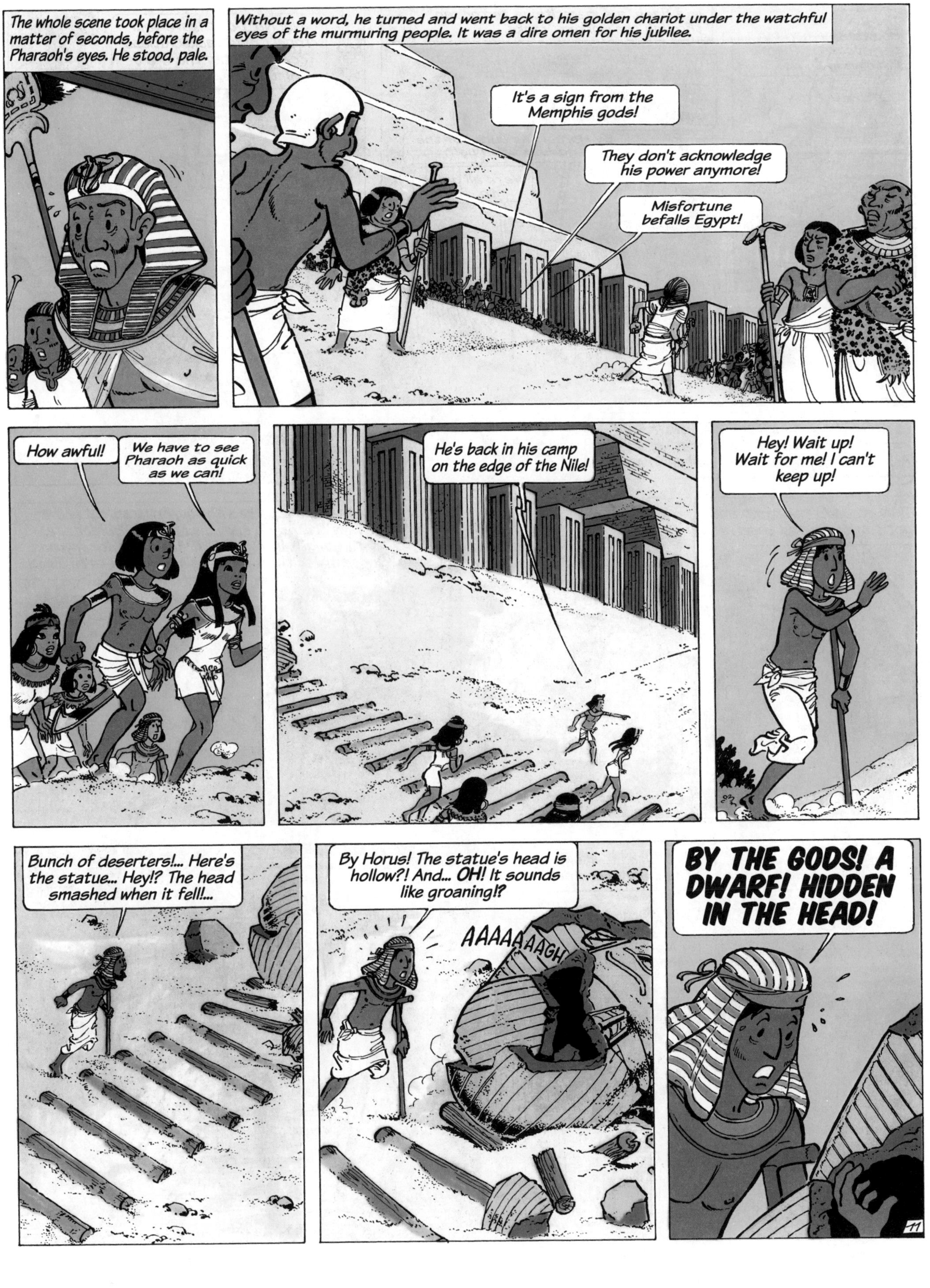
The whole scene took place in a matter of seconds, before the Pharaoh's eyes. He stood, pale.
Without a word, he turned and went back to his golden chariot under the watchful eyes of the murmuring people. It was a dire omen for his jubilee.
It's a sign from the Memphis gods!
They don't acknowledge his power anymore!
Misfortune befalls Egypt!
How awful!
We have to see Pharaoh as quick as we can!
He's back in his camp on the edge of the Nile!
Hey! Wait up! Wait for me! I can't keep up!
Bunch of deserters!... Here's the statue... Hey!? The head smashed when it fell!...
By Horus! The statue's head is hollow?! And... OH! It sounds like groaning!?
AAAAAAAGH
BY THE GODS! A DWARF! HIDDEN IN THE HEAD!
11

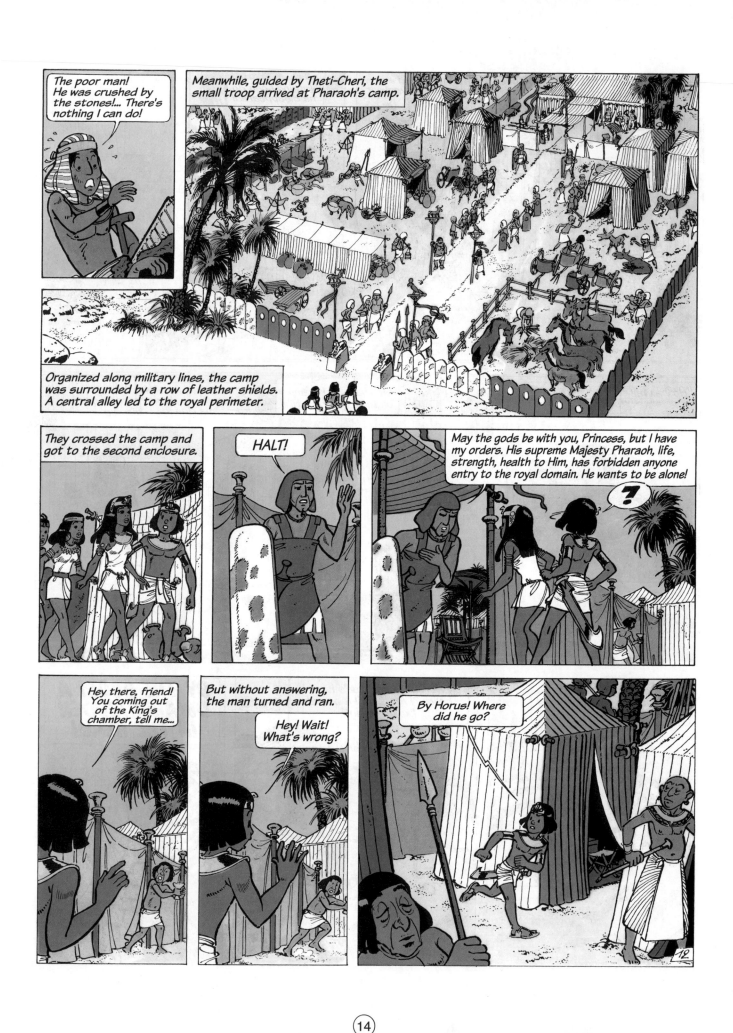

The poor man! He was crushed by the stones!... There's nothing I can do!

Meanwhile, guided by Theti-Cheri, the small troop arrived at Pharaoh's camp.

Organized along military lines, the camp was surrounded by a row of leather shields. A central alley led to the royal perimeter.

They crossed the camp and got to the second enclosure.

HALT!

May the gods be with you, Princess, but I have my orders. His supreme Majesty Pharaoh, life, strength, health to Him, has forbidden anyone entry to the royal domain. He wants to be alone!

?

Hey there, friend! You coming out of the King's chamber, tell me...

But without answering, the man turned and ran.

Hey! Wait! What's wrong?

By Horus! Where did he go?

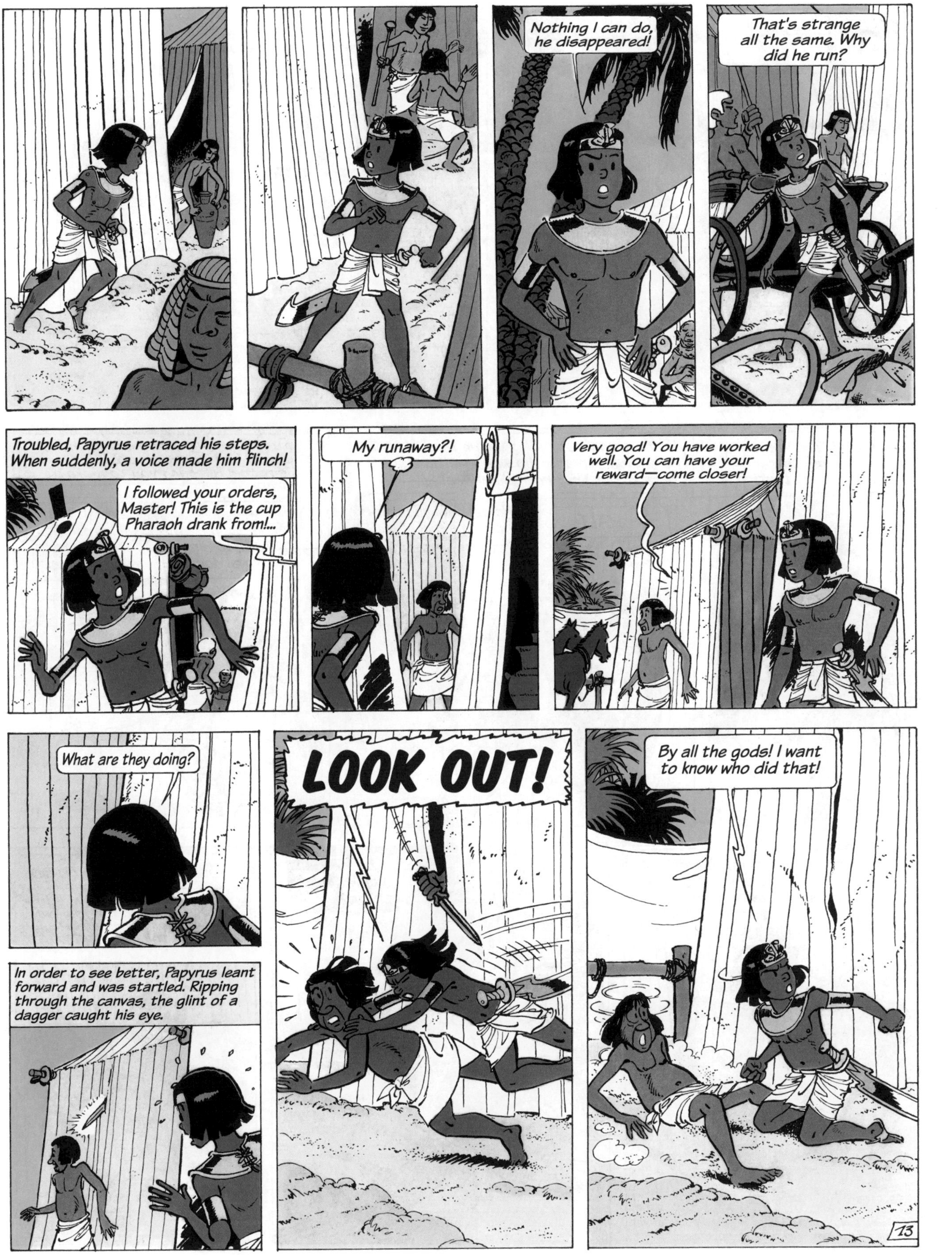
Nothing I can do, he disappeared!
That's strange all the same. Why did he run?
Troubled, Papyrus retraced his steps. When suddenly, a voice made him flinch!
I followed your orders, Master! This is the cup Pharaoh drank from!...
My runaway?!
Very good! You have worked well. You can have your reward—come closer!
What are they doing?
In order to see better, Papyrus leant forward and was startled. Ripping through the canvas, the glint of a dagger caught his eye.
LOOK OUT!
By all the gods! I want to know who did that!
13

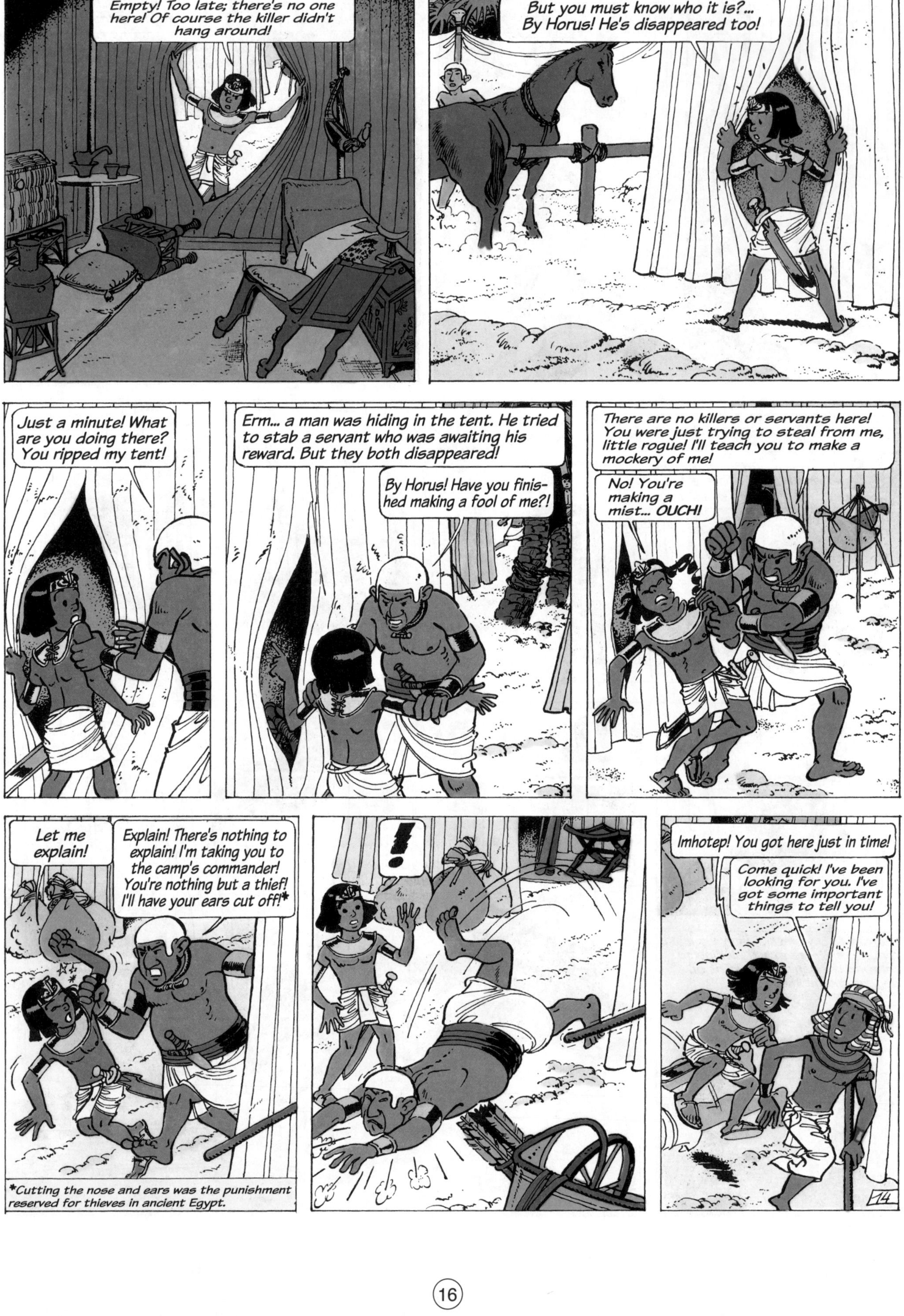
Empty! Too late; there's no one here! Of course the killer didn't hang around!
But you must know who it is?... By Horus! He's disappeared too!
Just a minute! What are you doing there? You ripped my tent!
Erm... a man was hiding in the tent. He tried to stab a servant who was awaiting his reward. But they both disappeared!
By Horus! Have you finished making a fool of me?!
There are no killers or servants here! You were just trying to steal from me, little rogue! I'll teach you to make a mockery of me!
No! You're making a mist... OUCH!
Let me explain!
Explain! There's nothing to explain! I'm taking you to the camp's commander! You're nothing but a thief! I'll have your ears cut off!*
*Cutting the nose and ears was the punishment reserved for thieves in ancient Egypt.
!
Imhotep! You got here just in time!
Come quick! I've been looking for you. I've got some important things to tell you!
14

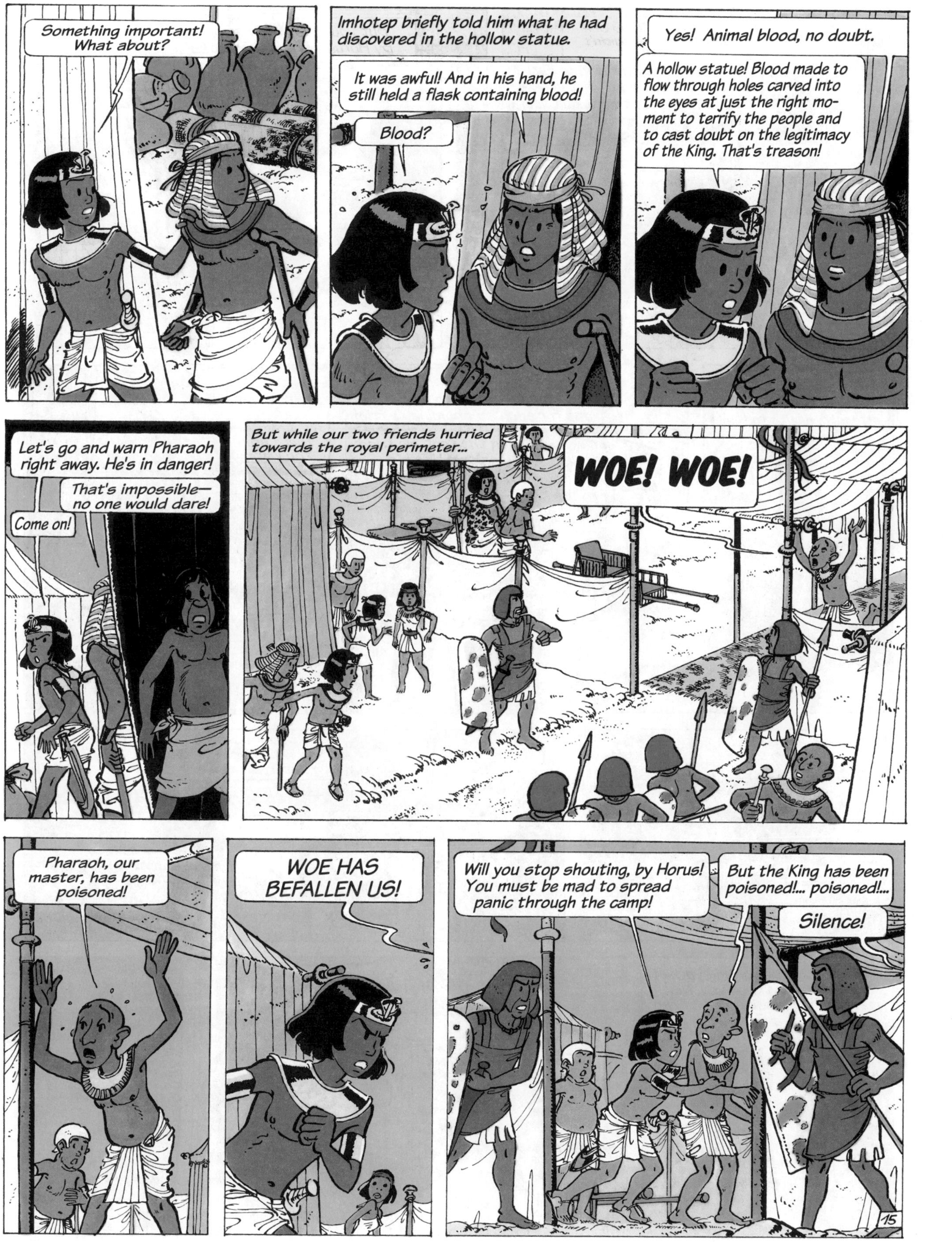
Something important! What about?
Imhotep briefly told him what he had discovered in the hollow statue.
It was awful! And in his hand, he still held a flask containing blood!
Blood?
Yes! Animal blood, no doubt.
A hollow statue! Blood made to flow through holes carved into the eyes at just the right moment to terrify the people and to cast doubt on the legitimacy of the King. That's treason!
Let's go and warn Pharaoh right away. He's in danger!
That's impossible— no one would dare!
Come on!
But while our two friends hurried towards the royal perimeter...
WOE! WOE!
Pharaoh, our master, has been poisoned!
WOE HAS BEFALLEN US!
Will you stop shouting, by Horus! You must be mad to spread panic through the camp!
But the King has been poisoned!... poisoned!...
Silence!
15

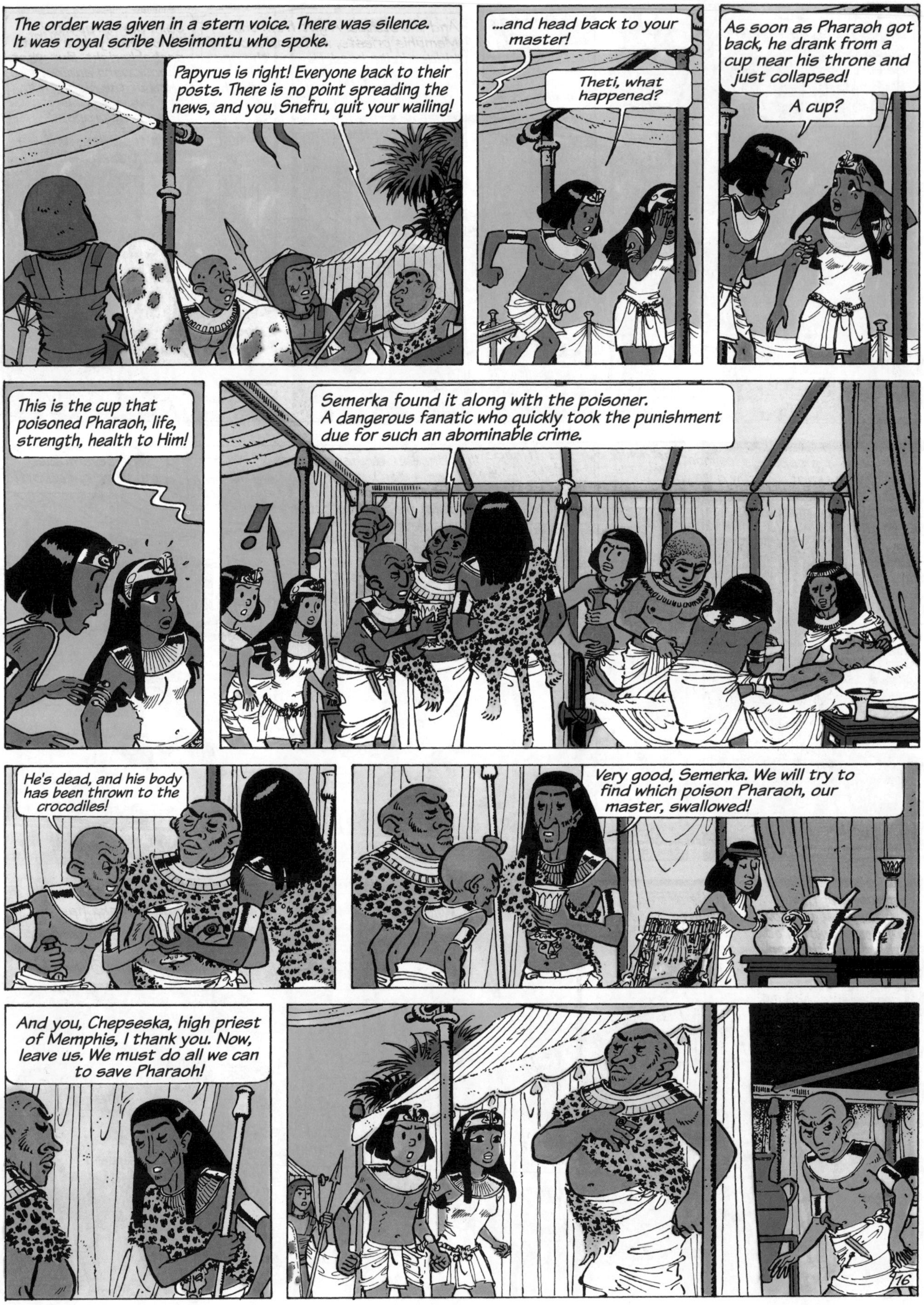

The order was given in a stern voice. There was silence. It was royal scribe Nesimontu who spoke.
Papyrus is right! Everyone back to their posts. There is no point spreading the news, and you, Snefru, quit your wailing!
...and head back to your master!
Theti, what happened?
As soon as Pharaoh got back, he drank from a cup near his throne and just collapsed!
A cup?
This is the cup that poisoned Pharaoh, life, strength, health to Him!
Semerka found it along with the poisoner. A dangerous fanatic who quickly took the punishment due for such an abominable crime.
He's dead, and his body has been thrown to the crocodiles!
Very good, Semerka. We will try to find which poison Pharaoh, our master, swallowed!
And you, Chepseska, high priest of Memphis, I thank you. Now, leave us. We must do all we can to save Pharaoh!
16

By Ra! That's outrageous! One of Semerka's servants stole Pharaoh's cup. He isn't dead!... I managed to save him from his master's dagger!... I recognized that dagger; it was there on Semerka's belt!

And the statue! A gift from the Memphis priests, we found a dwarf hidden in its head. He was the one that made the blood run from the statue's eyes. He's dead!... It's a plot against the King, and the guilty parties have just left!

Calm down, Papyrus! I know you; you're most probably right. But what is your word against the word of the high priest of Ptah, Memphis' greatest prophet?

Anyway, it's too late. The plot has succeeded!

Nesimontu??... How dare you! You deserve punishment!

Easy now! Noble princess, we have no proof of Chepseska's treason. I don't think that Pharaoh's life is in danger. But tomorrow he won't be able to preside over Heb Sed, his Jubilee celebration!

The ceremonies must be called off!

Impossible! The Jubilee date is sacred, and the King must show that he is still capable of firmly holding power. Tomorrow, in front of the clergy, the army and the people, he has to run three times around the perimeter traced out by the priests' markers on the great esplanade at the foot of the pyramid. Since the great pharaoh Djoser, this ritual test has not changed. The King has to succeed, or else...

Or else?

Or else he'll be declared incapable and will have to choose a co-regent. Chepseska has royal blood and is Memphis' foremost prophet. After the broken statue incident that drove the people into a frenzy, he'll have no trouble taking the throne!

So all is lost!

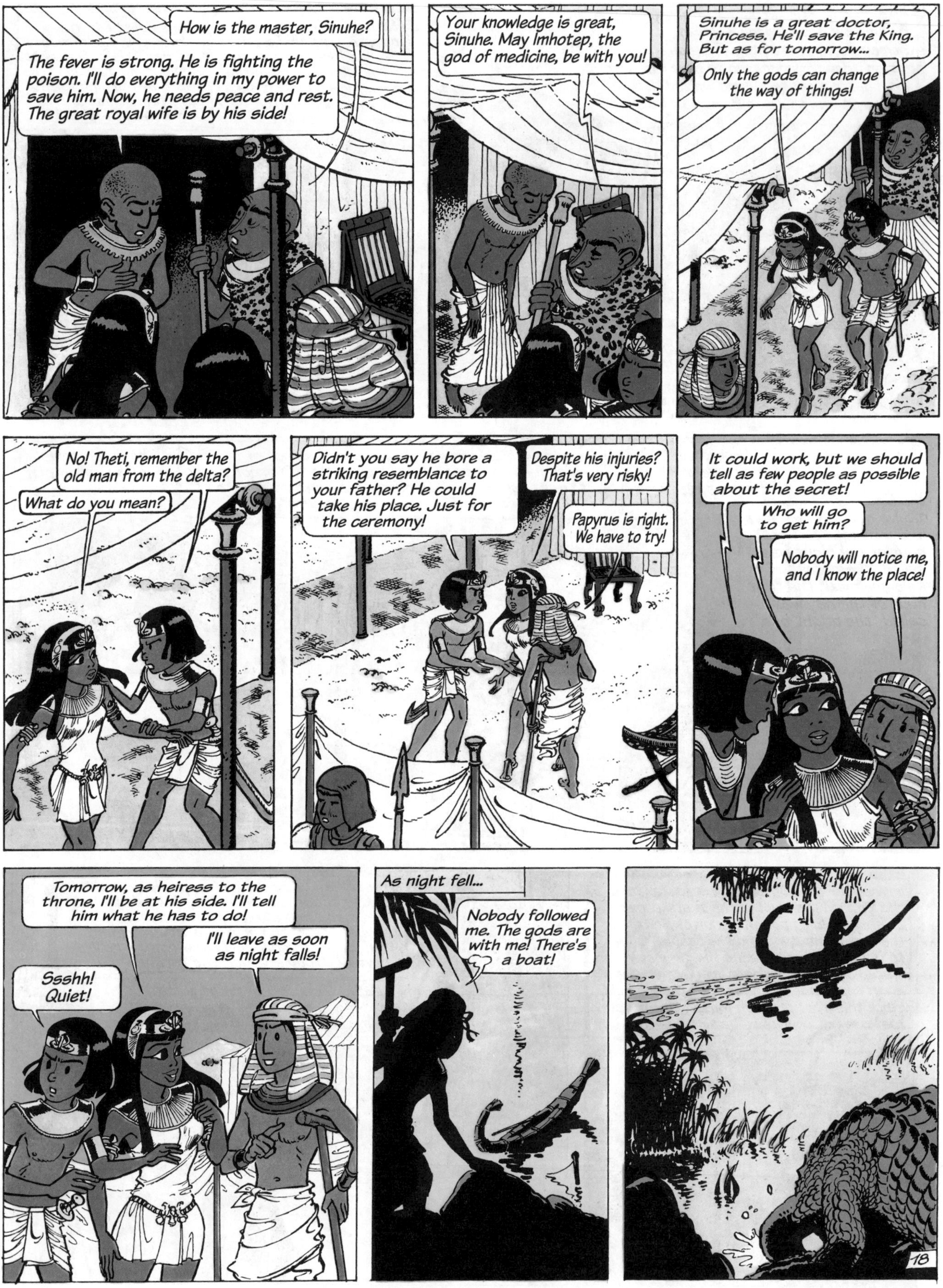
How is the master, Sinuhe?
The fever is strong. He is fighting the poison. I'll do everything in my power to save him. Now, he needs peace and rest. The great royal wife is by his side!
Your knowledge is great, Sinuhe. May Imhotep, the god of medicine, be with you!
Sinuhe is a great doctor, Princess. He'll save the King. But as for tomorrow...
Only the gods can change the way of things!
What do you mean?
No! Theti, remember the old man from the delta?
Didn't you say he bore a striking resemblance to your father? He could take his place. Just for the ceremony!
Despite his injuries? That's very risky!
Papyrus is right. We have to try!
It could work, but we should tell as few people as possible about the secret!
Who will go to get him?
Nobody will notice me, and I know the place!
Tomorrow, as heiress to the throne, I'll be at his side. I'll tell him what he has to do!
I'll leave as soon as night falls!
Ssshh! Quiet!
As night fell...
Nobody followed me. The gods are with me! There's a boat!
18

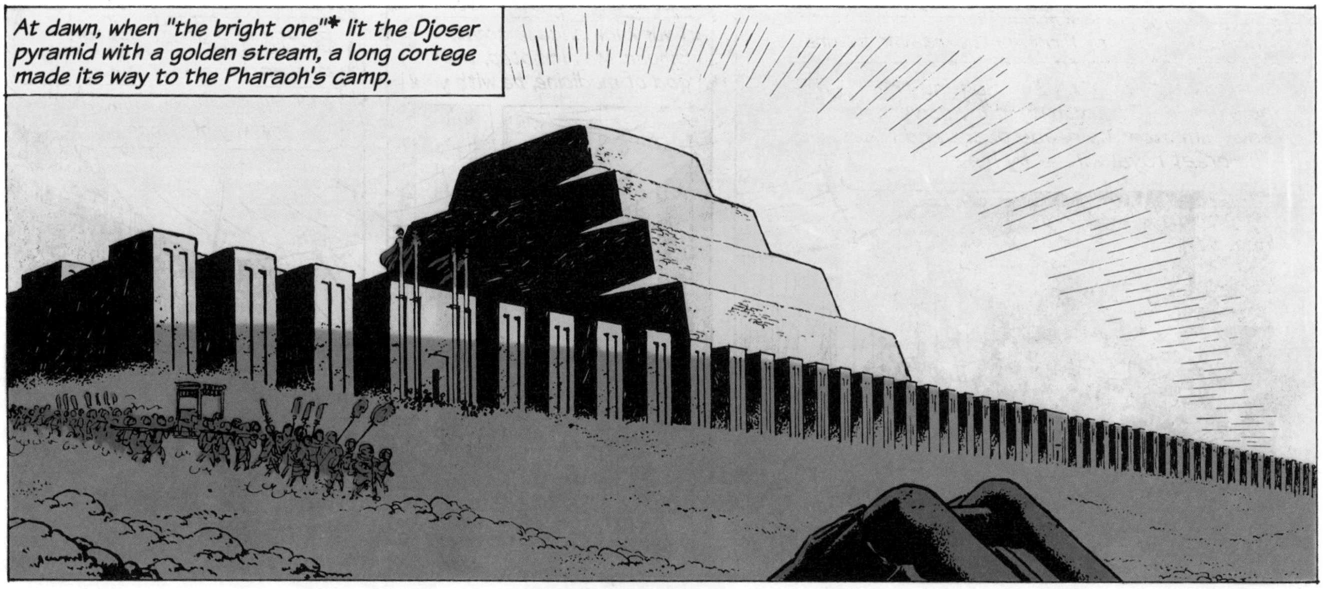
At dawn, when "the bright one"* lit the Djoser pyramid with a golden stream, a long cortege made its way to the Pharaoh's camp.

*The Egyptians divided the day and night into twelve hours. Every hour had a name. The first hour of the night was called "the defeat of Ra's enemies"; the first hour of the day was called "the bright one."

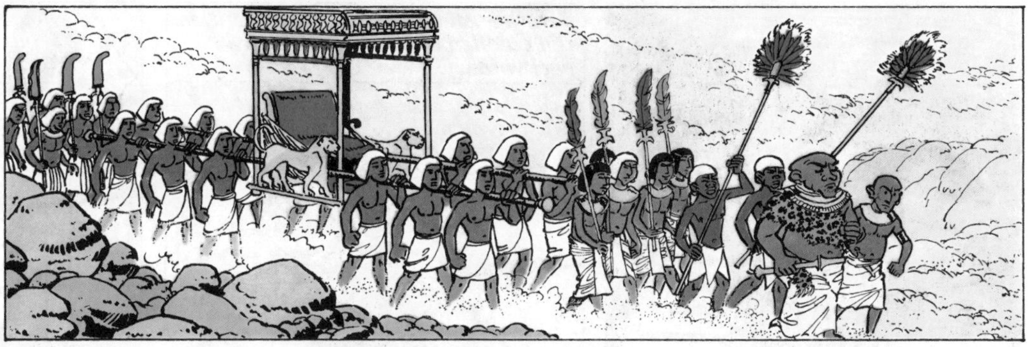

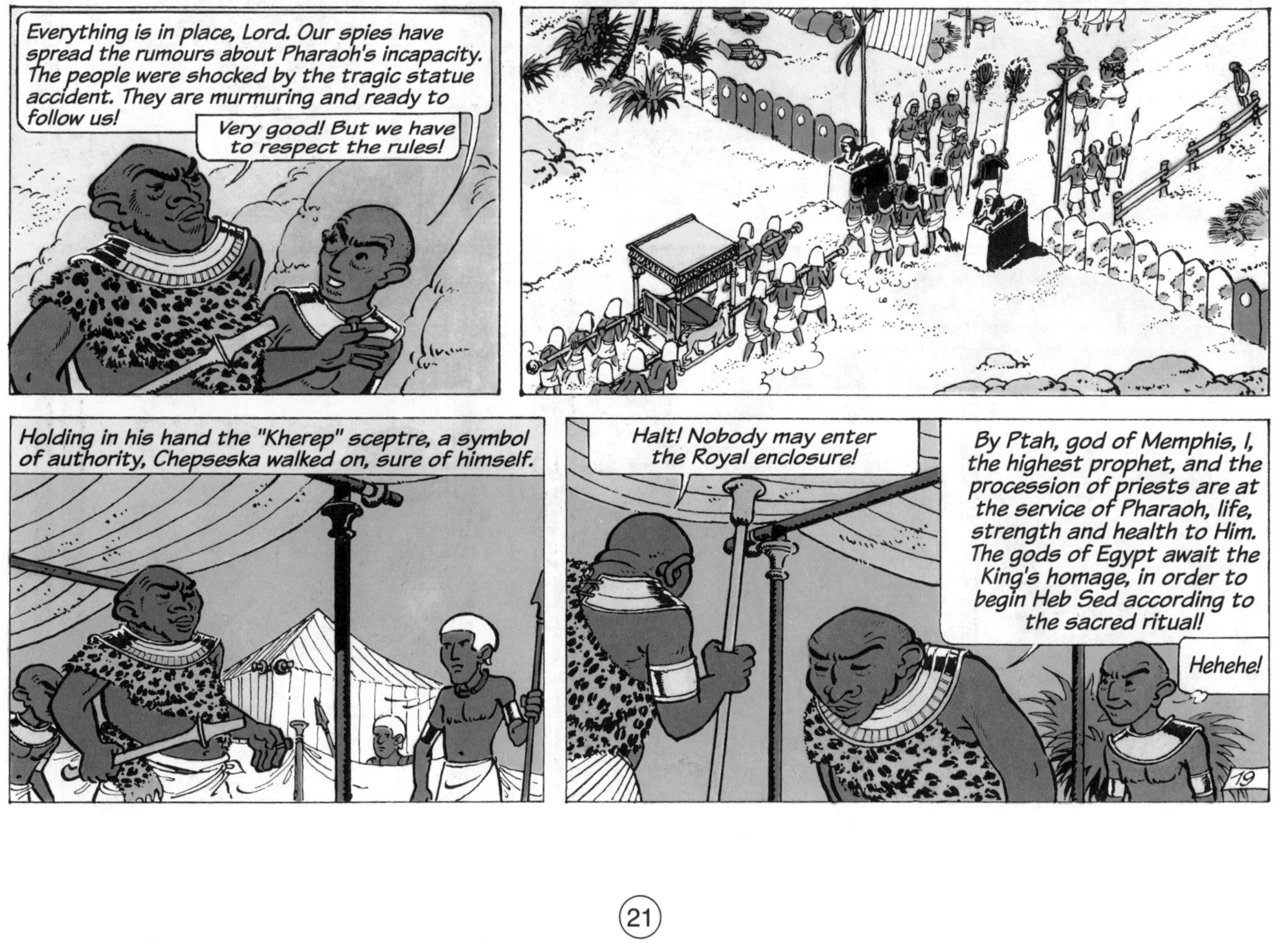
Everything is in place, Lord. Our spies have spread the rumours about Pharaoh's incapacity. The people were shocked by the tragic statue accident. They are murmuring and ready to follow us!
Very good! But we have to respect the rules!
Holding in his hand the "Kherep" sceptre, a symbol of authority, Chepseska walked on, sure of himself.
Halt! Nobody may enter the Royal enclosure!
By Ptah, god of Memphis, I, the highest prophet, and the procession of priests are at the service of Pharaoh, life, strength and health to Him. The gods of Egypt await the King's homage, in order to begin Heb Sed according to the sacred ritual!
Hehehe!
19

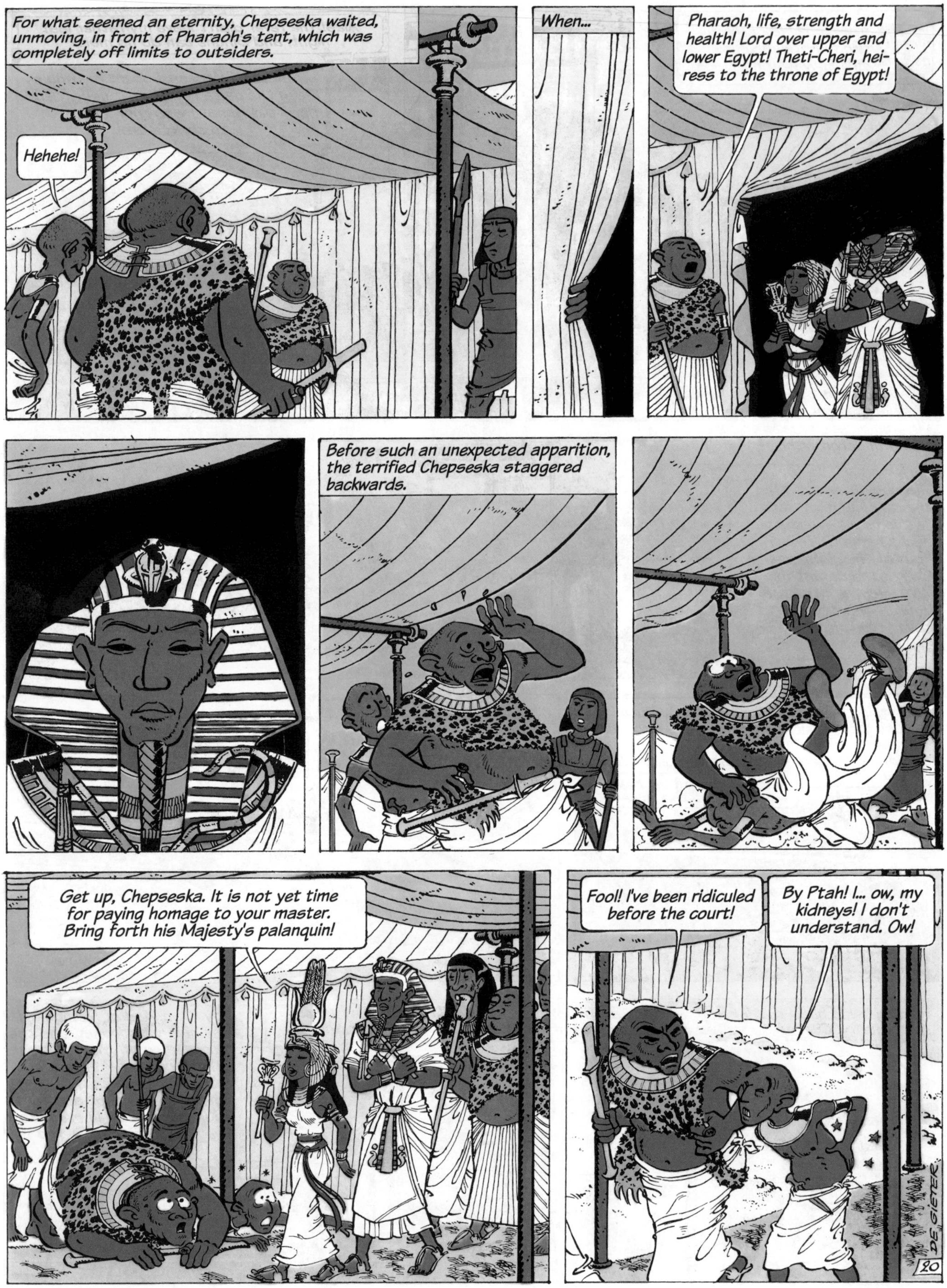
For what seemed an eternity, Chepseska waited, unmoving, in front of Pharaoh's tent, which was completely off limits to outsiders.
Hehehe!
When...
Pharaoh, life, strength and health! Lord over upper and lower Egypt! Theti-Cheri, heiress to the throne of Egypt!
Before such an unexpected apparition, the terrified Chepseska staggered backwards.
Get up, Chepseska. It is not yet time for paying homage to your master. Bring forth his Majesty's palanquin!
Fool! I've been ridiculed before the court!
By Ptah! I... ow, my kidneys! I don't understand. Ow!
DE GIETER
20

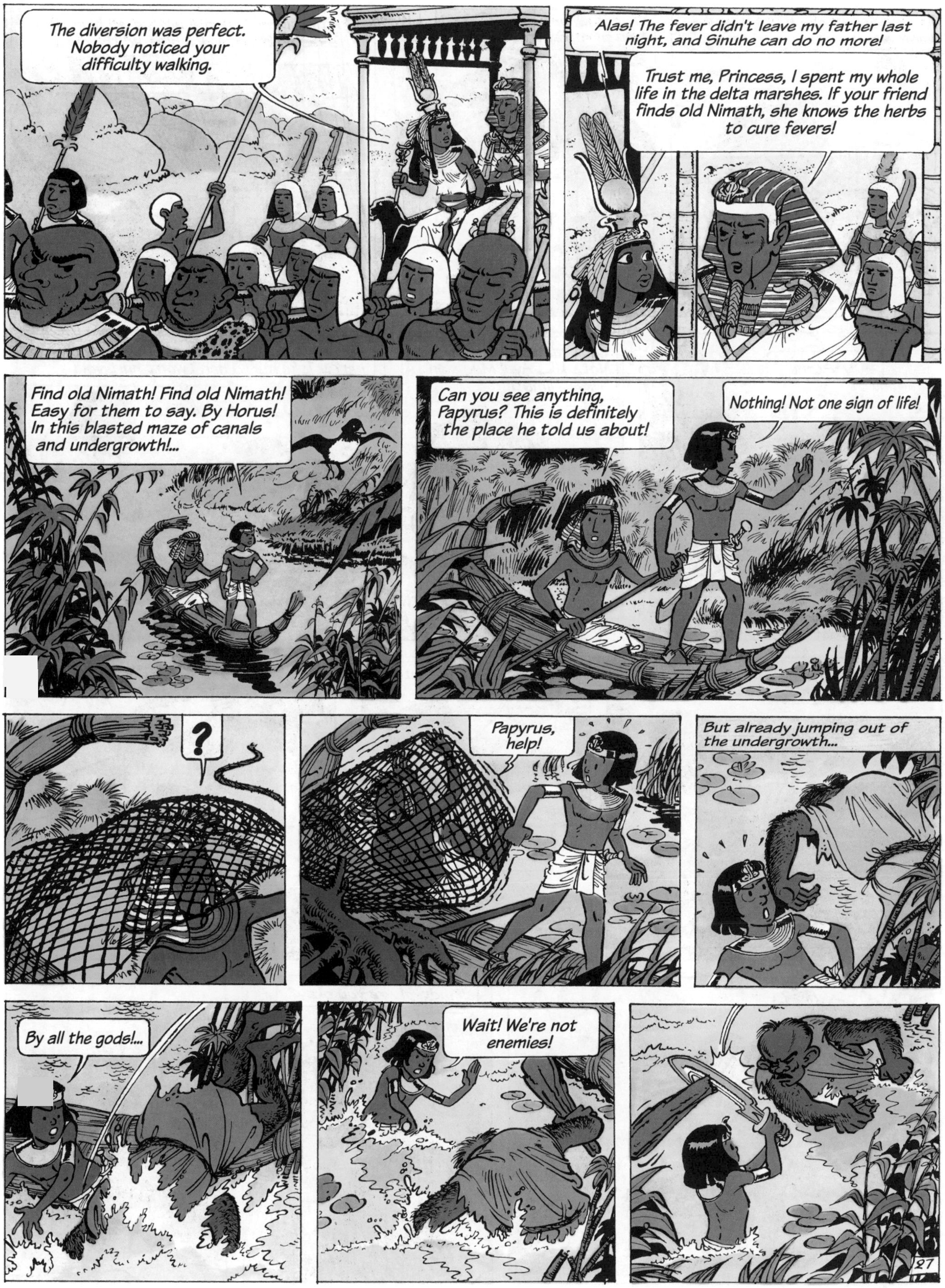
The diversion was perfect. Nobody noticed your difficulty walking.
Alas! The fever didn't leave my father last night, and Sinuhe can do no more!
Trust me, Princess, I spent my whole life in the delta marshes. If your friend finds old Nimath, she knows the herbs to cure fevers!
Find old Nimath! Find old Nimath! Easy for them to say. By Horus! In this blasted maze of canals and undergrowth!...
Can you see anything, Papyrus? This is definitely the place he told us about!
Nothing! Not one sign of life!
?
Papyrus, help!
But already jumping out of the undergrowth...
By all the gods!...
Wait! We're not enemies!
27

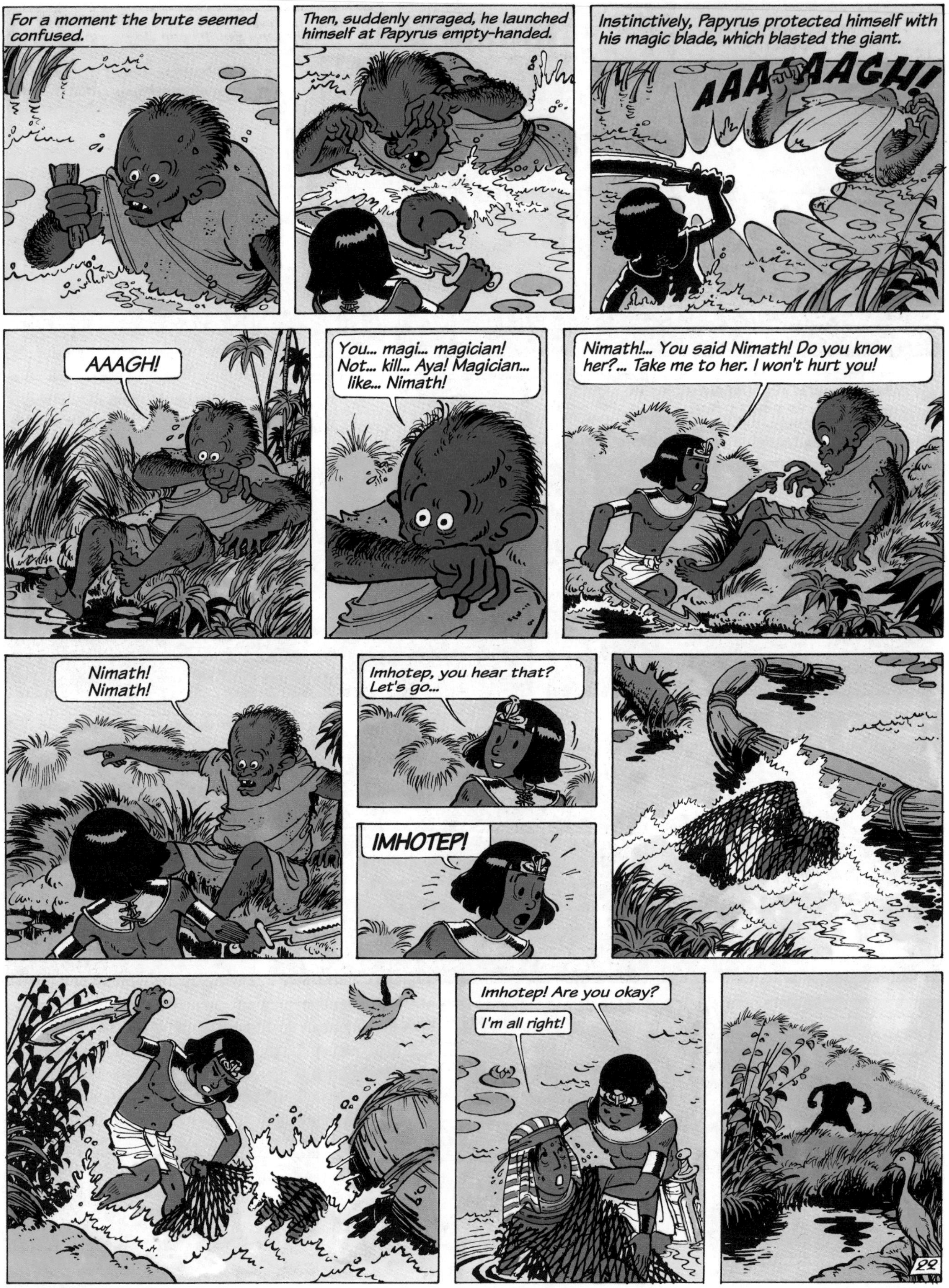

For a moment the brute seemed confused.
Then, suddenly enraged, he launched himself at Papyrus empty-handed.
Instinctively, Papyrus protected himself with his magic blade, which blasted the giant.
AAAAAAGH!
AAAGH!
You... magi... magician! Not... kill... Aya! Magician... like... Nimath!
Nimath!... You said Nimath! Do you know her?... Take me to her. I won't hurt you!
Nimath! Nimath!
Imhotep, you hear that? Let's go...
IMHOTEP!
Imhotep! Are you okay?
I'm all right!

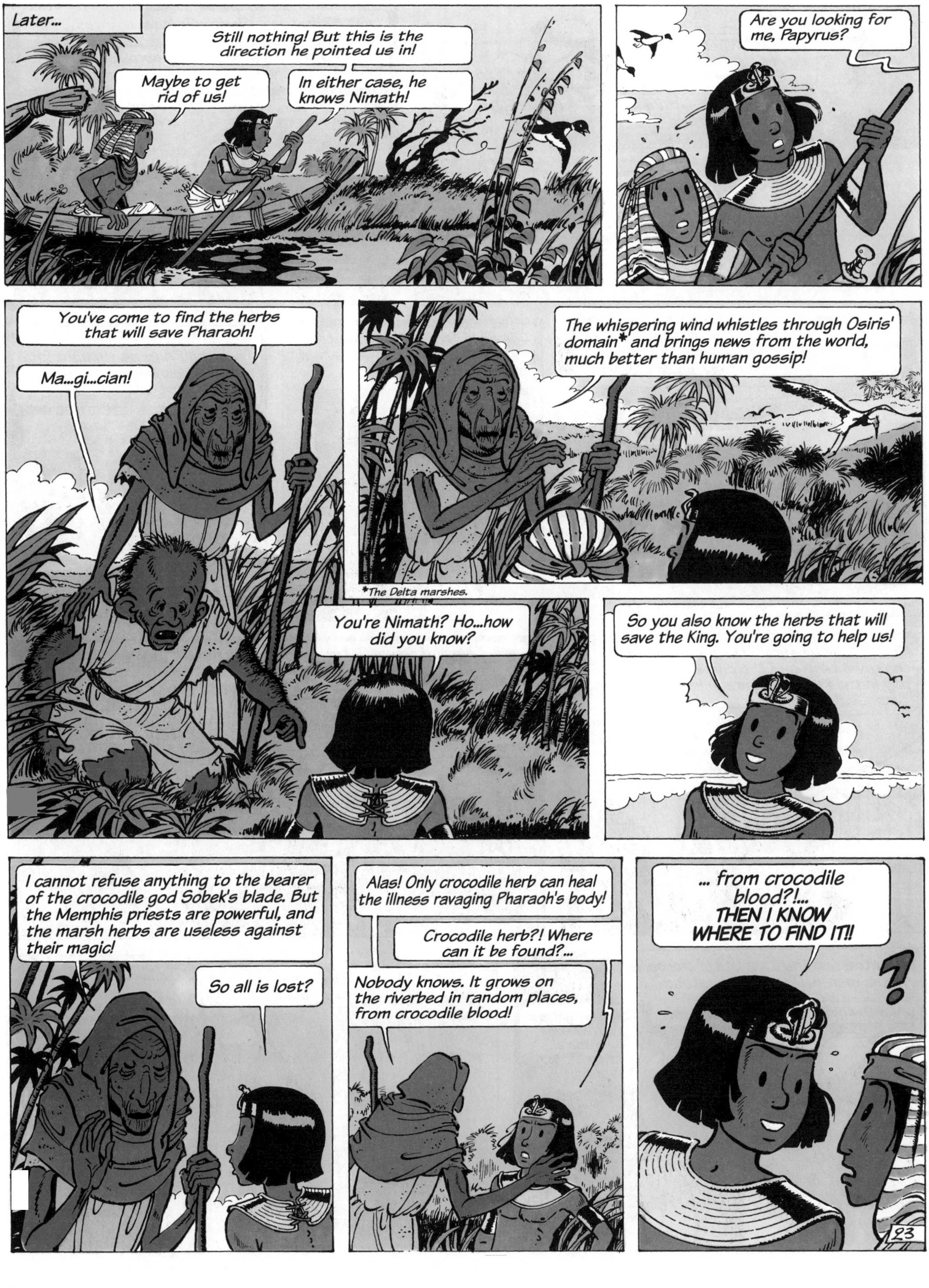
Later...
Still nothing! But this is the direction he pointed us in!
Maybe to get rid of us!
In either case, he knows Nimath!
Are you looking for me, Papyrus?
You've come to find the herbs that will save Pharaoh!
Ma...gi...cian!
The whispering wind whistles through Osiris' domain* and brings news from the world, much better than human gossip!
*The Delta marshes.
You're Nimath? Ho...how did you know?
So you also know the herbs that will save the King. You're going to help us!
I cannot refuse anything to the bearer of the crocodile god Sobek's blade. But the Memphis priests are powerful, and the marsh herbs are useless against their magic!
So all is lost?
Alas! Only crocodile herb can heal the illness ravaging Pharaoh's body!
Crocodile herb?! Where can it be found?...
Nobody knows. It grows on the riverbed in random places, from crocodile blood!
... from crocodile blood?!...
THEN I KNOW WHERE TO FIND IT!!
?
23

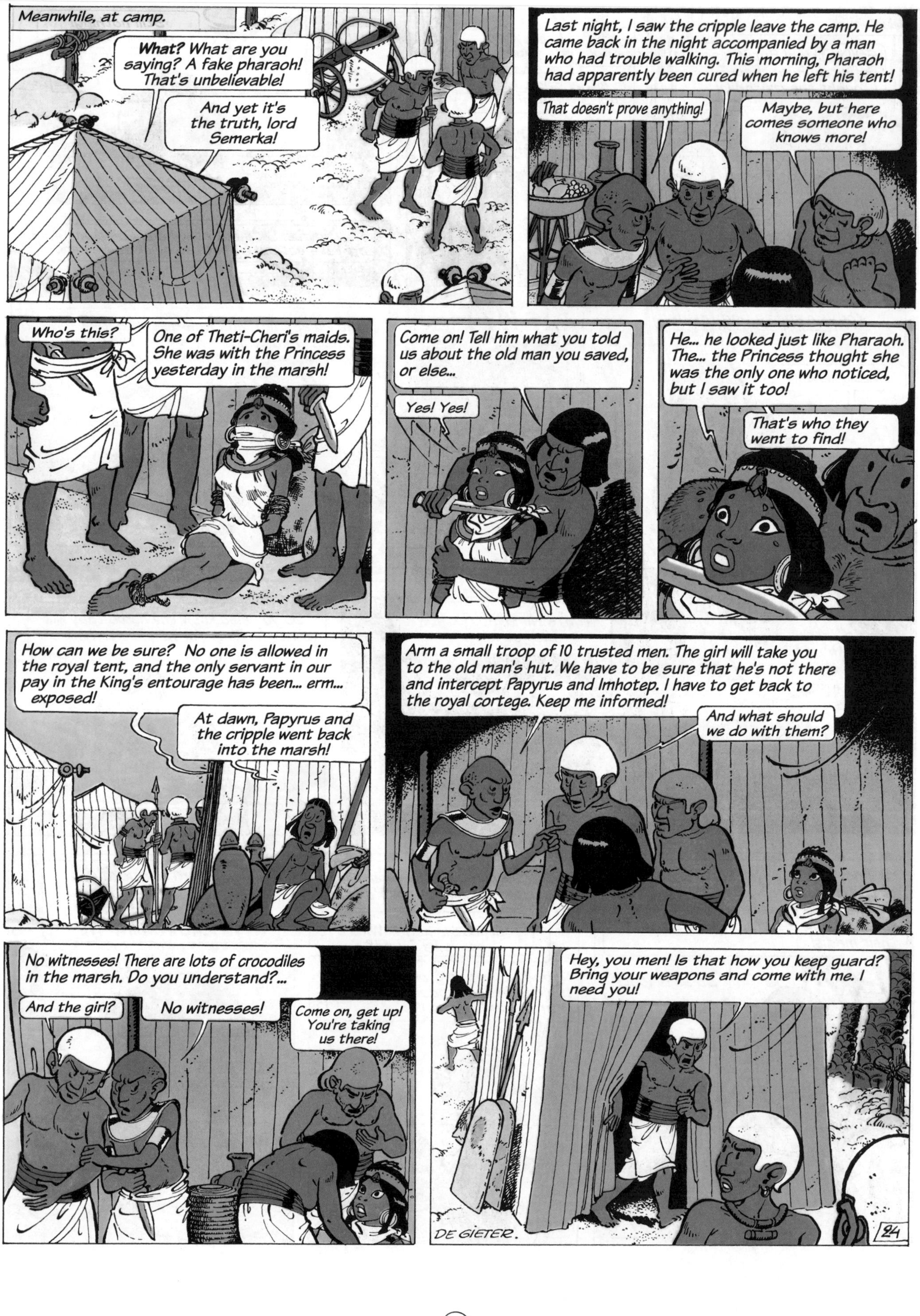
Meanwhile, at camp.
What? What are you saying? A fake pharaoh! That's unbelievable!
And yet it's the truth, lord Semerka!
Last night, I saw the cripple leave the camp. He came back in the night accompanied by a man who had trouble walking. This morning, Pharaoh had apparently been cured when he left his tent!
That doesn't prove anything!
Maybe, but here comes someone who knows more!
Who's this?
One of Theti-Cheri's maids. She was with the Princess yesterday in the marsh!
Come on! Tell him what you told us about the old man you saved, or else...
Yes! Yes!
He... he looked just like Pharaoh. The... the Princess thought she was the only one who noticed, but I saw it too!
That's who they went to find!
How can we be sure? No one is allowed in the royal tent, and the only servant in our pay in the King's entourage has been... erm... exposed!
At dawn, Papyrus and the cripple went back into the marsh!
Arm a small troop of 10 trusted men. The girl will take you to the old man's hut. We have to be sure that he's not there and intercept Papyrus and Imhotep. I have to get back to the royal cortege. Keep me informed!
And what should we do with them?
No witnesses! There are lots of crocodiles in the marsh. Do you understand?...
And the girl?
No witnesses!
Come on, get up! You're taking us there!
Hey, you men! Is that how you keep guard? Bring your weapons and come with me. I need you!
DE GIETER.
24

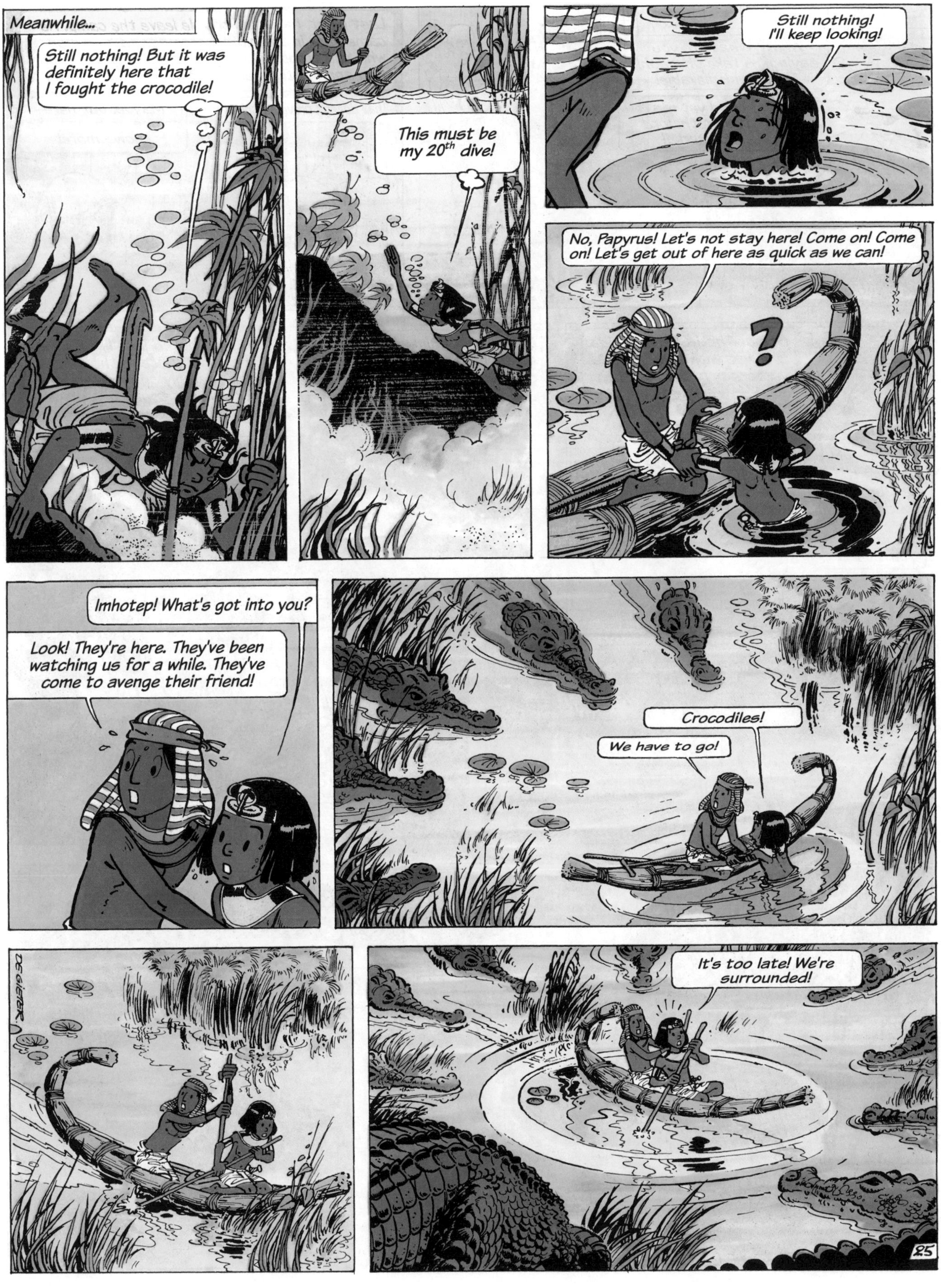
Meanwhile...
Still nothing! But it was definitely here that I fought the crocodile!
This must be my 20th dive!
Still nothing! I'll keep looking!
No, Papyrus! Let's not stay here! Come on! Come on! Let's get out of here as quick as we can!
Imhotep! What's got into you?
Look! They're here. They've been watching us for a while. They've come to avenge their friend!
Crocodiles!
We have to go!
It's too late! We're surrounded!
25

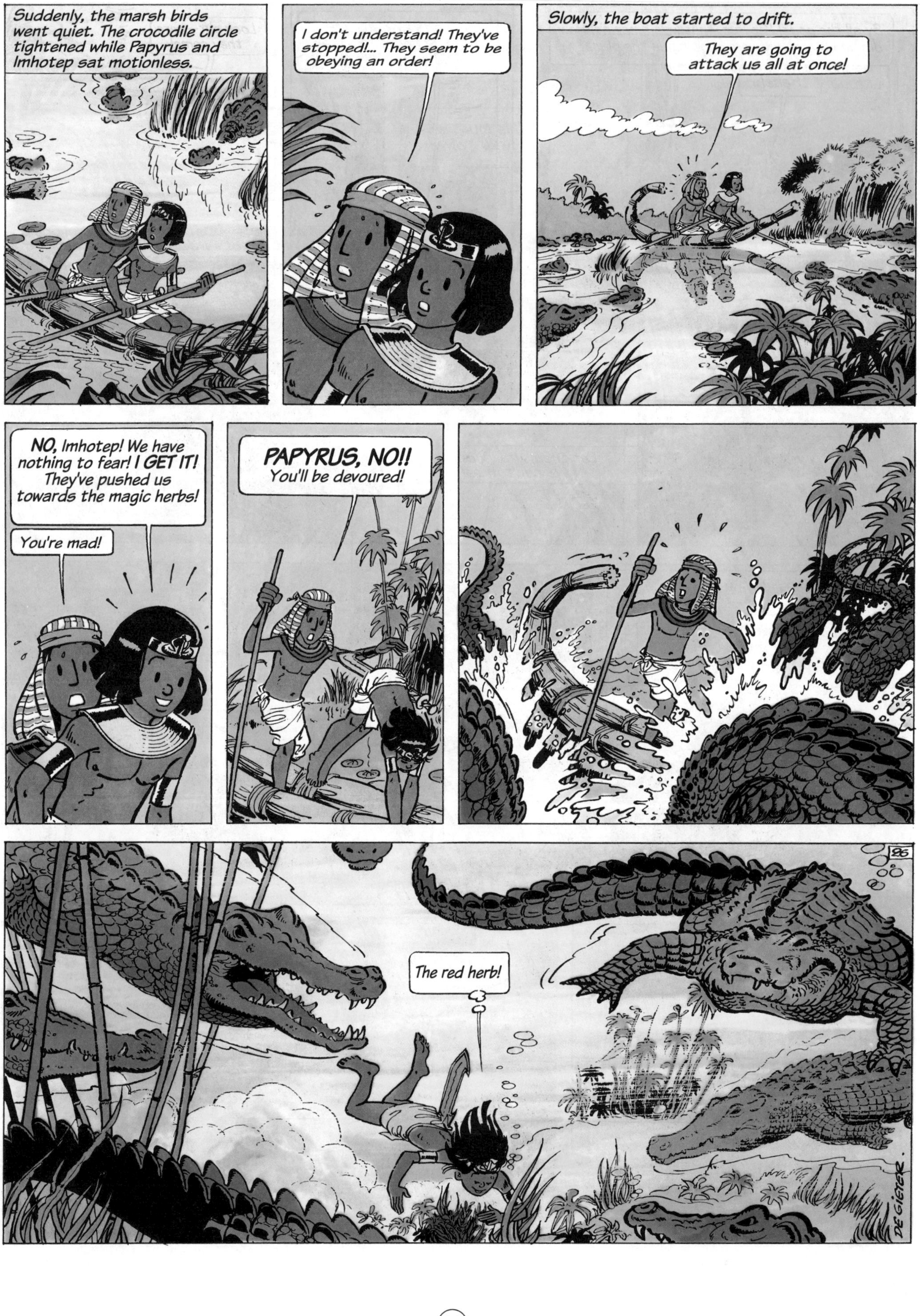
Suddenly, the marsh birds went quiet. The crocodile circle tightened while Papyrus and Imhotep sat motionless.
I don't understand! They've stopped!... They seem to be obeying an order!
Slowly, the boat started to drift.
They are going to attack us all at once!
NO, Imhotep! We have nothing to fear! I GET IT! They've pushed us towards the magic herbs!
You're mad!
PAPYRUS, NO!! You'll be devoured!
The red herb!
DE GIETER.

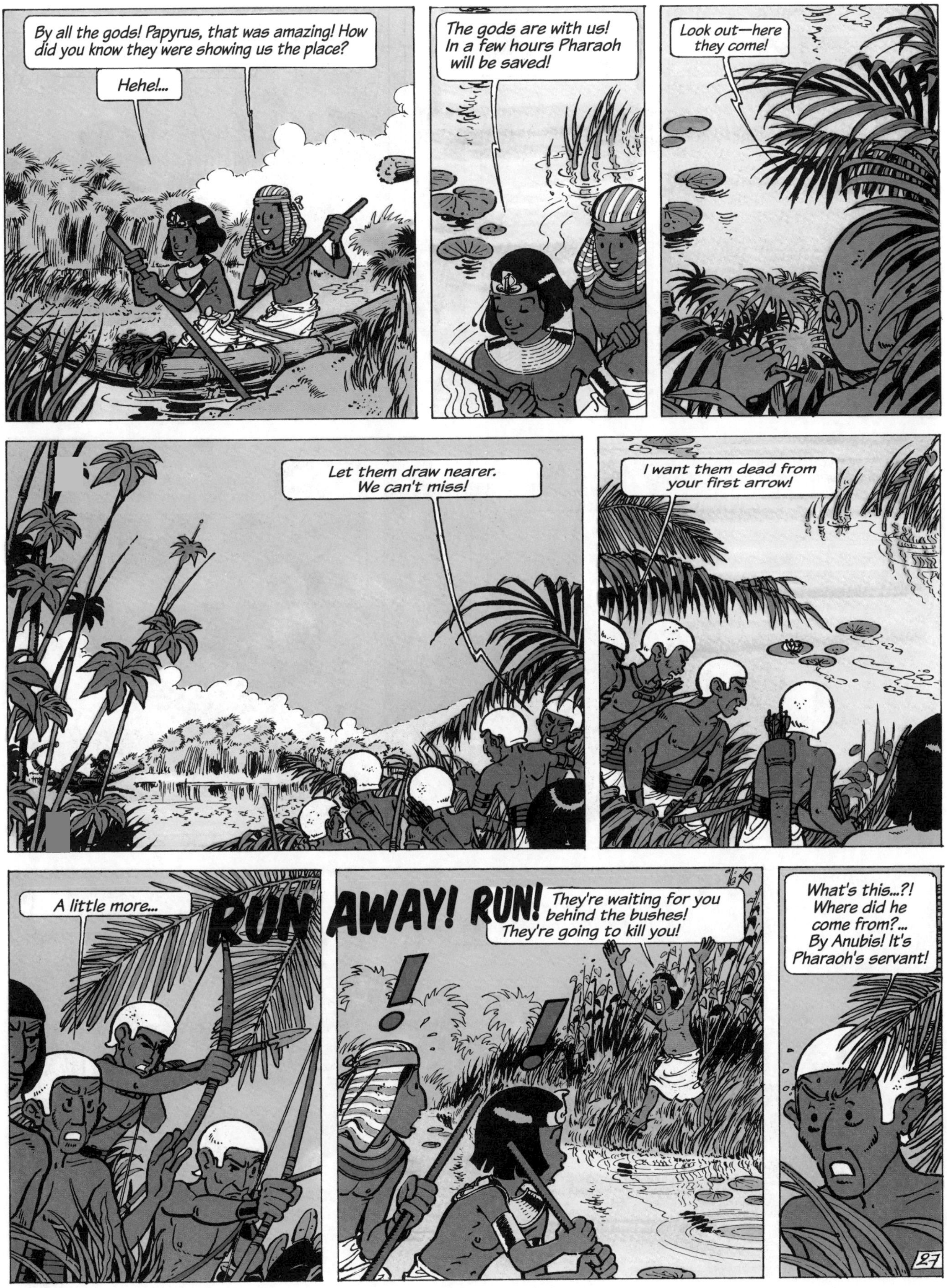
By all the gods! Papyrus, that was amazing! How did you know they were showing us the place?
Hehe!...
The gods are with us! In a few hours Pharaoh will be saved!
Look out—here they come!
Let them draw nearer. We can't miss!
I want them dead from your first arrow!
A little more...
RUN AWAY! RUN!
They're waiting for you behind the bushes! They're going to kill you!
!
!
What's this...?! Where did he come from?... By Anubis! It's Pharaoh's servant!
27

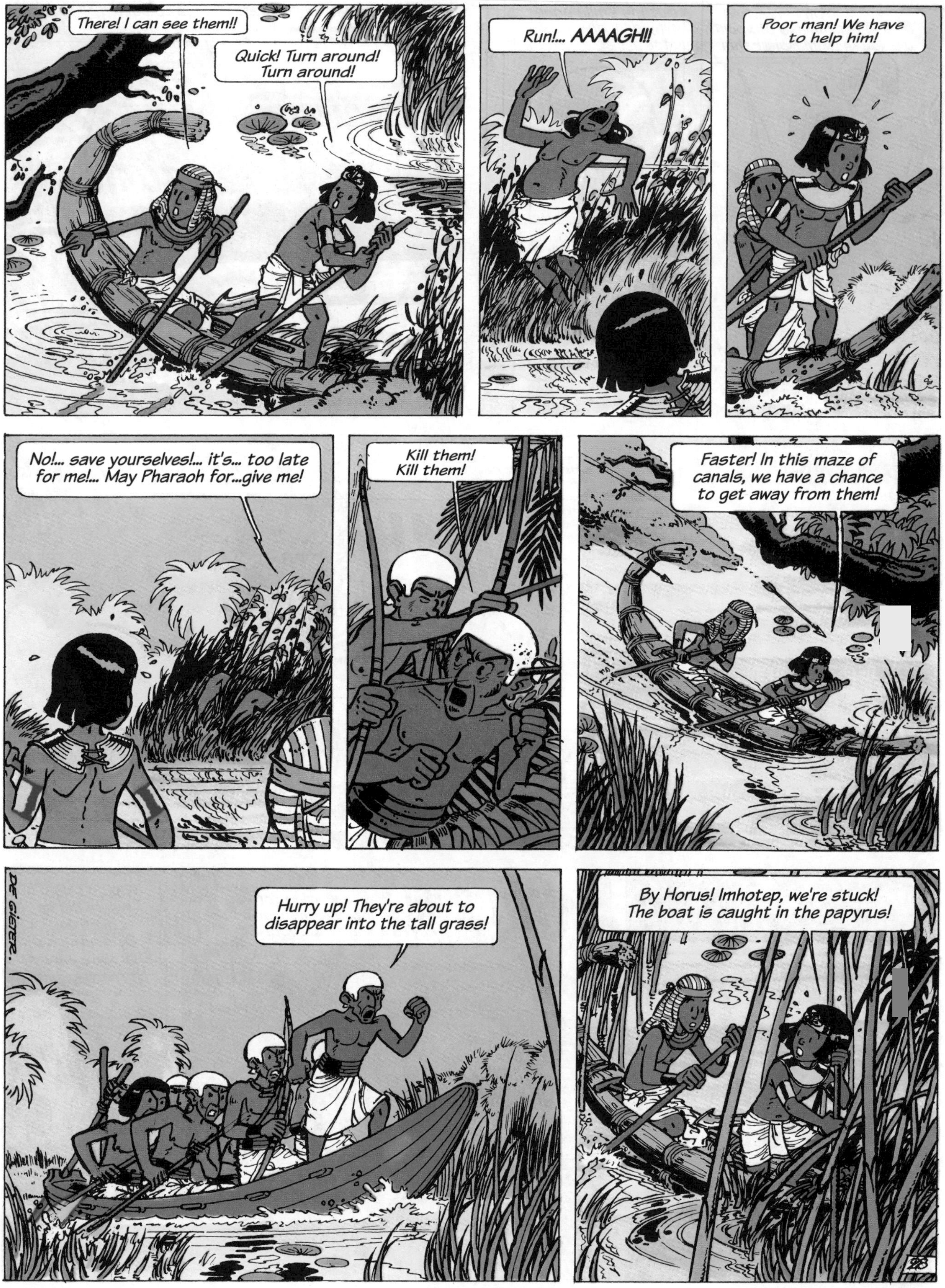
There! I can see them!!
Quick! Turn around! Turn around!
Run!... AAAAGH!!
Poor man! We have to help him!
No!... save yourselves!... it's... too late for me!... May Pharaoh for...give me!
Kill them! Kill them!
Faster! In this maze of canals, we have a chance to get away from them!
DE GIETER.
Hurry up! They're about to disappear into the tall grass!
By Horus! Imhotep, we're stuck! The boat is caught in the papyrus!

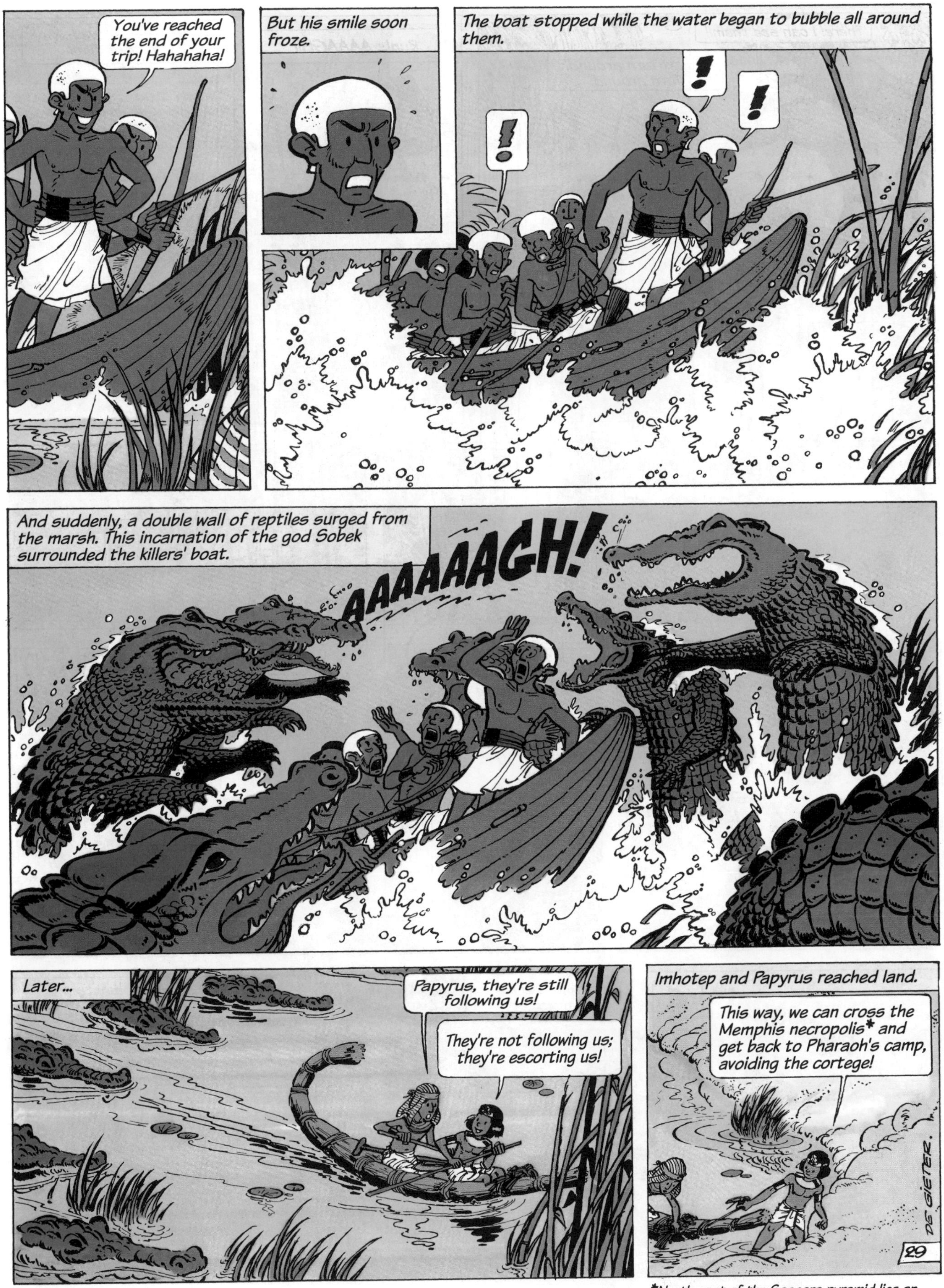
You've reached the end of your trip! Hahahaha!
But his smile soon froze.
The boat stopped while the water began to bubble all around them.
!
!
!
And suddenly, a double wall of reptiles surged from the marsh. This incarnation of the god Sobek surrounded the killers' boat.
AAAAAAGH!
Later...
Papyrus, they're still following us!
They're not following us; they're escorting us!
Imhotep and Papyrus reached land.
This way, we can cross the Memphis necropolis* and get back to Pharaoh's camp, avoiding the cortege!
DE GIETER
29

*North-east of the Saqqara pyramid lies an underground cemetery that covers several dozen hectares.

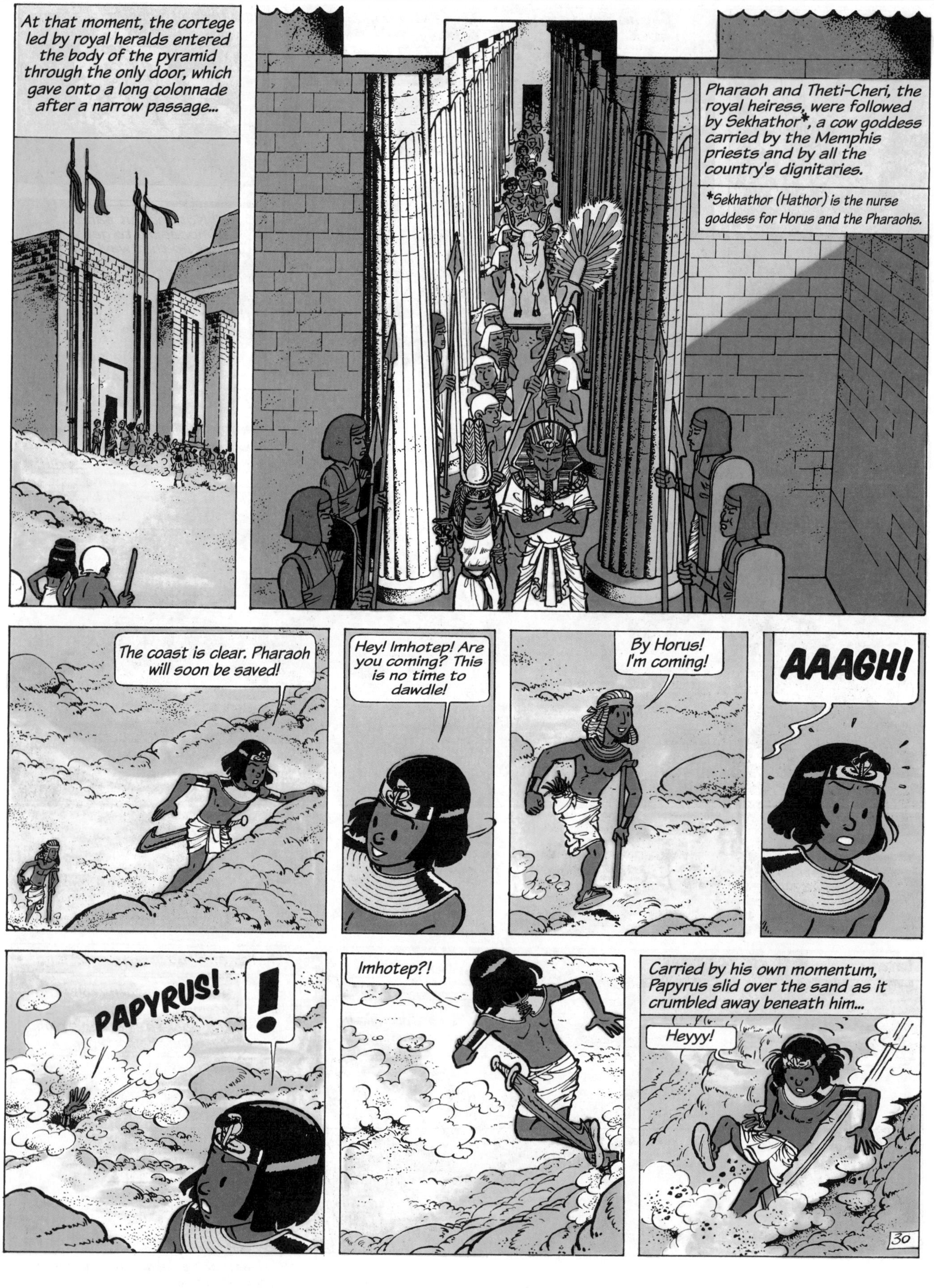
At that moment, the cortege led by royal heralds entered the body of the pyramid through the only door, which gave onto a long colonnade after a narrow passage...
Pharaoh and Theti-Cheri, the royal heiress, were followed by Sekhathor*, a cow goddess carried by the Memphis priests and by all the country's dignitaries.
*Sekhathor (Hathor) is the nurse goddess for Horus and the Pharaohs.
The coast is clear. Pharaoh will soon be saved!
Hey! Imhotep! Are you coming? This is no time to dawdle!
By Horus! I'm coming!
AAAGH!
PAPYRUS!
!
Imhotep?!
Carried by his own momentum, Papyrus slid over the sand as it crumbled away beneath him...
Heyyy!
30

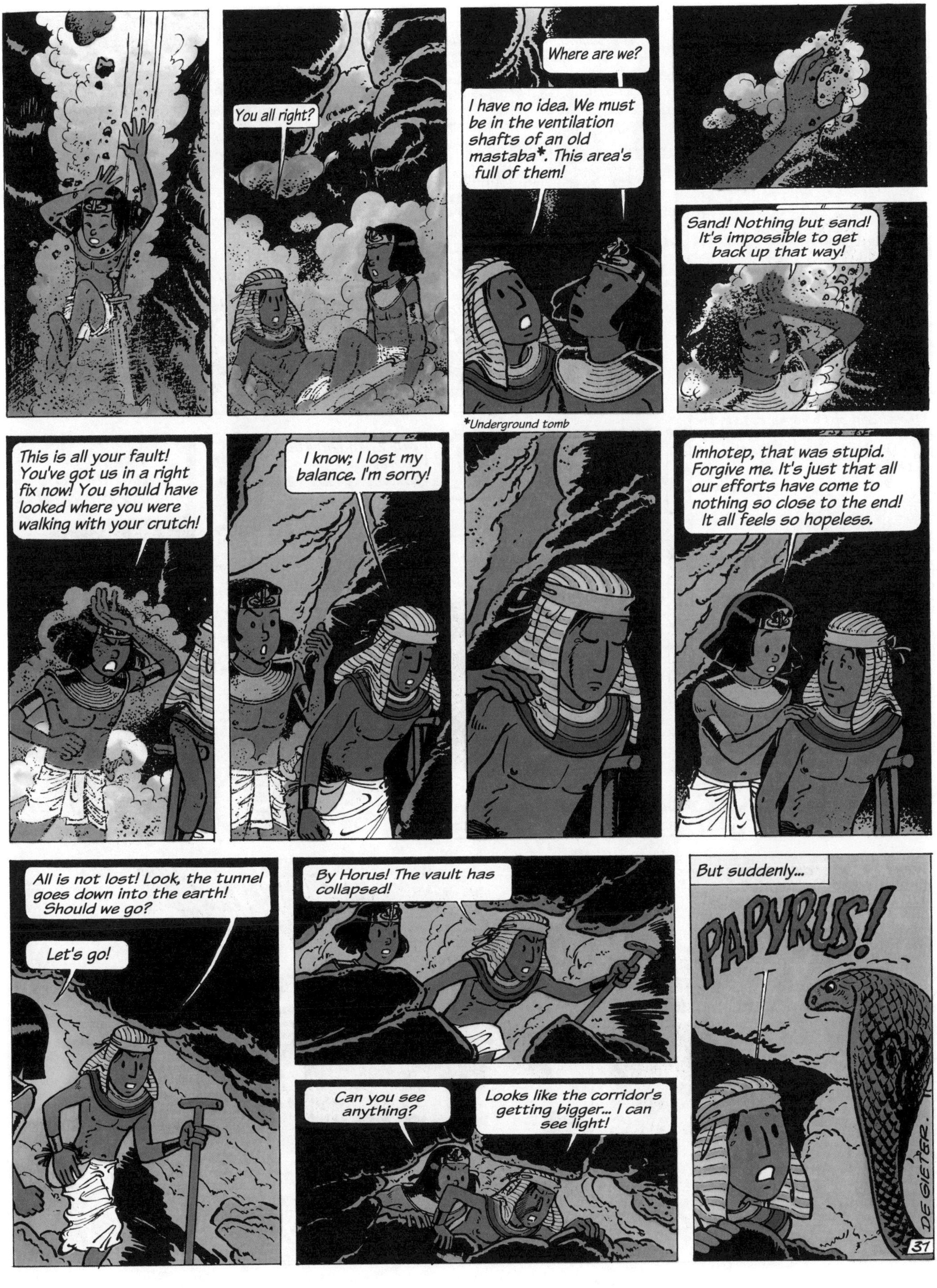
You all right?
Where are we?
I have no idea. We must be in the ventilation shafts of an old mastaba*. This area's full of them!
Sand! Nothing but sand! It's impossible to get back up that way!
*Underground tomb
This is all your fault! You've got us in a right fix now! You should have looked where you were walking with your crutch!
I know; I lost my balance. I'm sorry!
Imhotep, that was stupid. Forgive me. It's just that all our efforts have come to nothing so close to the end! It all feels so hopeless.
All is not lost! Look, the tunnel goes down into the earth! Should we go?
Let's go!
By Horus! The vault has collapsed!
Can you see anything?
Looks like the corridor's getting bigger... I can see light!
But suddenly...
PAPYRUS!
DE GIETER
31

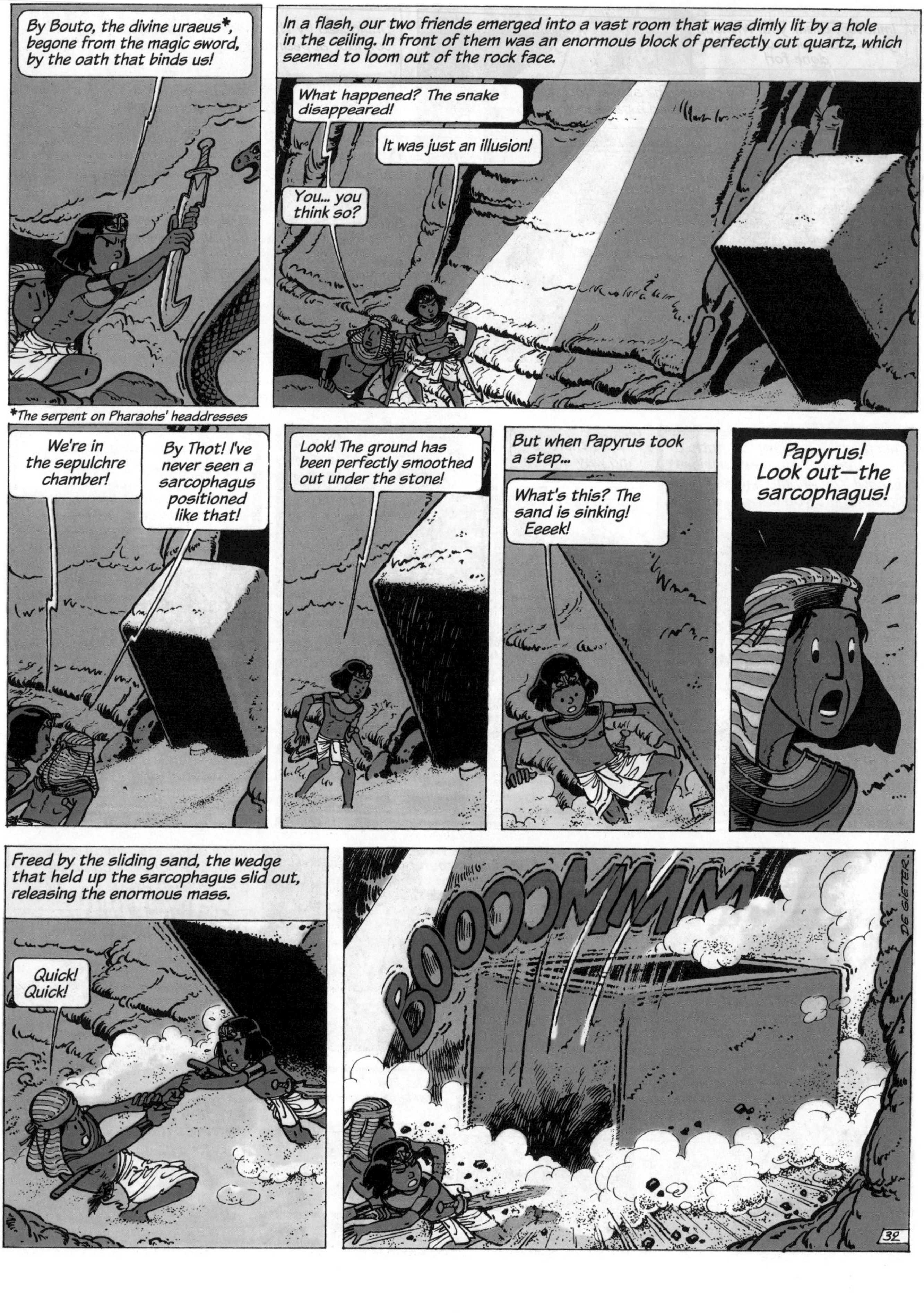
By Bouto, the divine uraeus*, begone from the magic sword, by the oath that binds us!
In a flash, our two friends emerged into a vast room that was dimly lit by a hole in the ceiling. In front of them was an enormous block of perfectly cut quartz, which seemed to loom out of the rock face.
What happened? The snake disappeared!
It was just an illusion!
You... you think so?
*The serpent on Pharaohs' headdresses
We're in the sepulchre chamber!
By Thot! I've never seen a sarcophagus positioned like that!
Look! The ground has been perfectly smoothed out under the stone!
But when Papyrus took a step...
What's this? The sand is sinking! Eeeek!
Papyrus! Look out—the sarcophagus!
Freed by the sliding sand, the wedge that held up the sarcophagus slid out, releasing the enormous mass.
Quick! Quick!
BOOOOMMMM
DE GIETER.
32

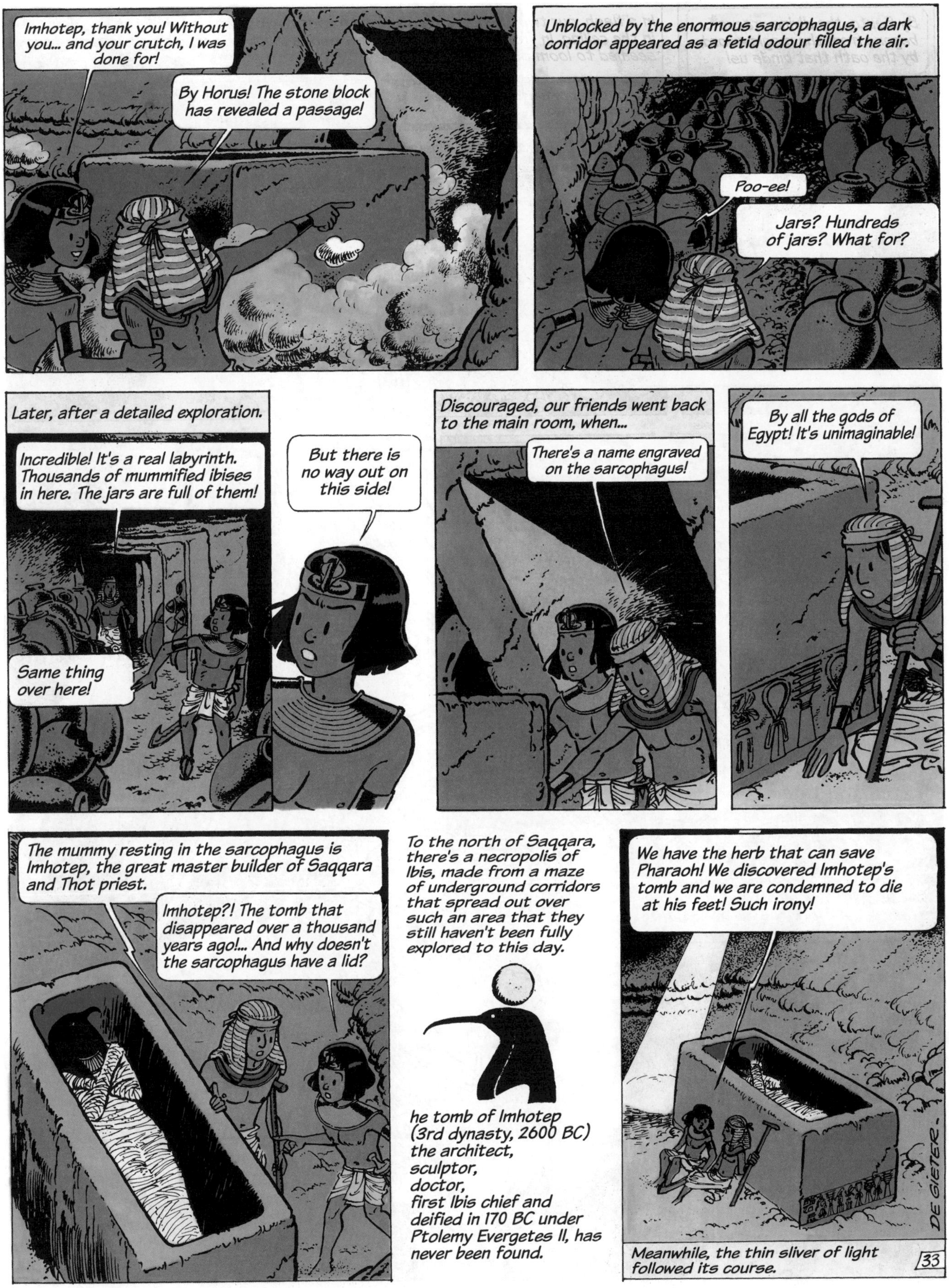
Imhotep, thank you! Without you... and your crutch, I was done for!
By Horus! The stone block has revealed a passage!
Unblocked by the enormous sarcophagus, a dark corridor appeared as a fetid odour filled the air.
Poo-ee!
Jars? Hundreds of jars? What for?
Later, after a detailed exploration.
Incredible! It's a real labyrinth. Thousands of mummified ibises in here. The jars are full of them!
Same thing over here!
But there is no way out on this side!
Discouraged, our friends went back to the main room, when...
There's a name engraved on the sarcophagus!
By all the gods of Egypt! It's unimaginable!
The mummy resting in the sarcophagus is Imhotep, the great master builder of Saqqara and Thot priest.
Imhotep?! The tomb that disappeared over a thousand years ago!... And why doesn't the sarcophagus have a lid?
To the north of Saqqara, there's a necropolis of Ibis, made from a maze of underground corridors that spread out over such an area that they still haven't been fully explored to this day.
he tomb of Imhotep (3rd dynasty, 2600 BC) the architect, sculptor, doctor, first Ibis chief and deified in 170 BC under Ptolemy Evergetes II, has never been found.
We have the herb that can save Pharaoh! We discovered Imhotep's tomb and we are condemned to die at his feet! Such irony!
DE GIETER.
Meanwhile, the thin sliver of light followed its course.
33

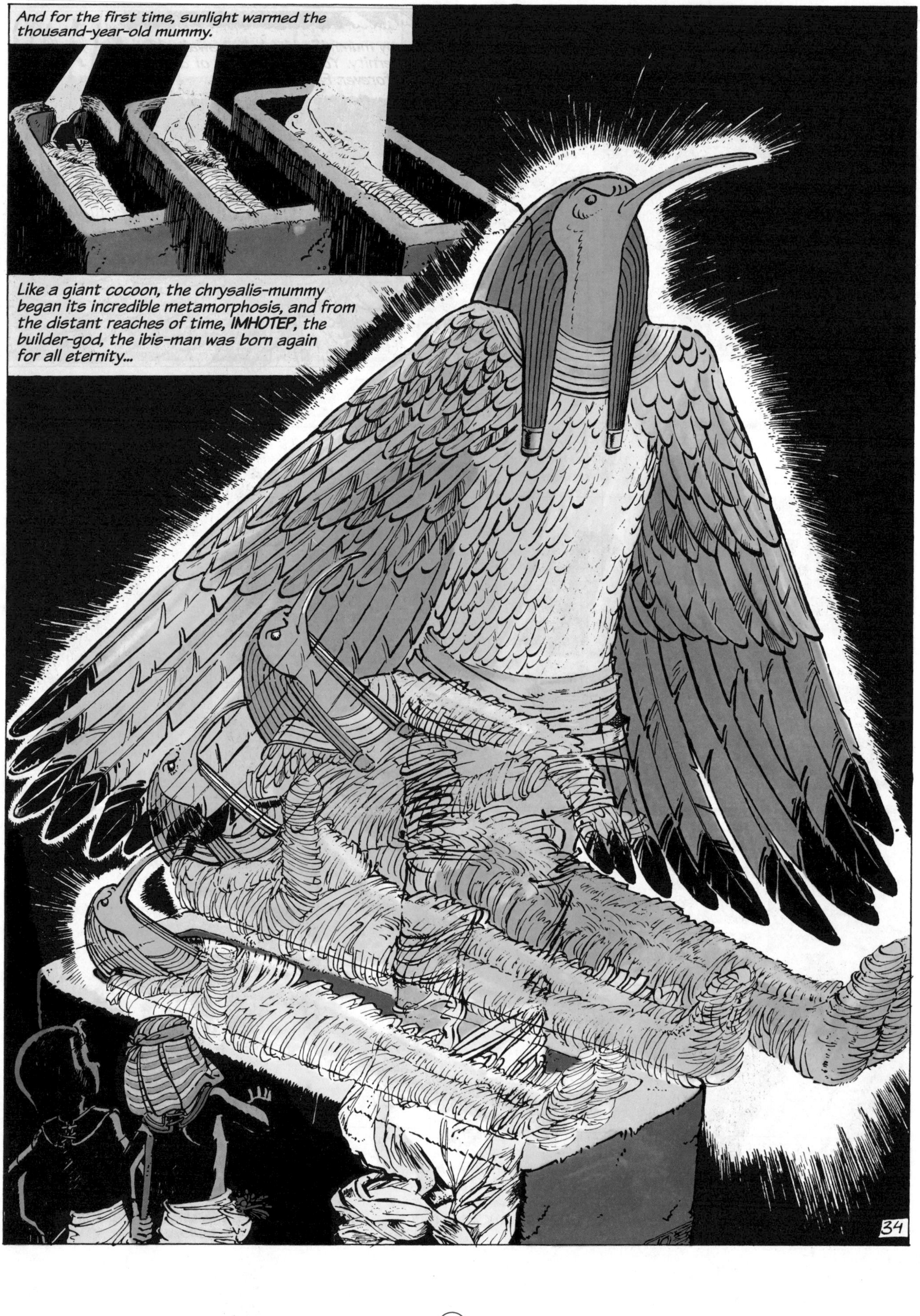
And for the first time, sunlight warmed the thousand-year-old mummy.
Like a giant cocoon, the chrysalis-mummy began its incredible metamorphosis, and from the distant reaches of time, IMHOTEP, the builder-god, the ibis-man was born again for all eternity...
34

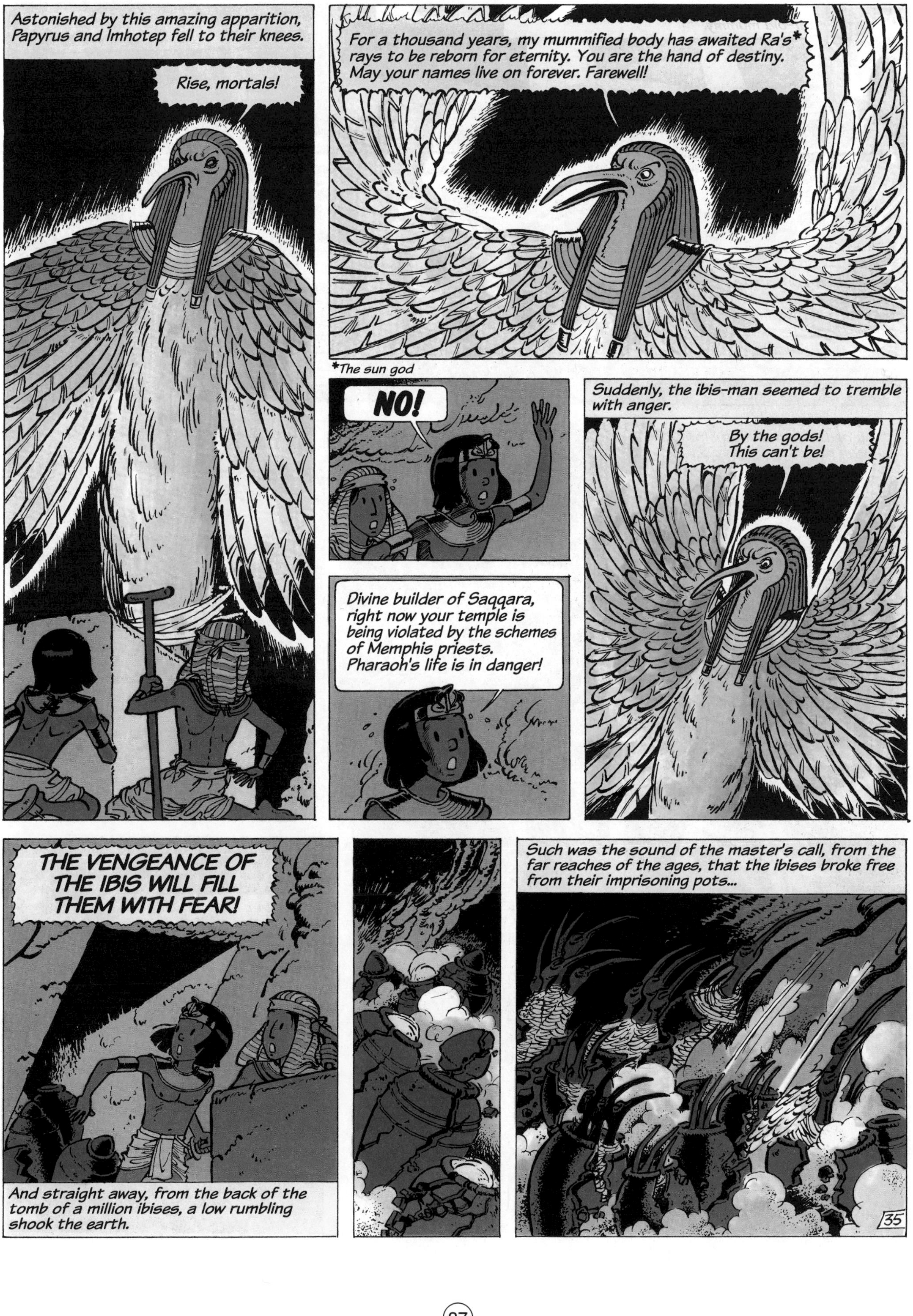

Astonished by this amazing apparition, Papyrus and Imhotep fell to their knees.
Rise, mortals!
For a thousand years, my mummified body has awaited Ra's* rays to be reborn for eternity. You are the hand of destiny. May your names live on forever. Farewell!
*The sun god
NO!
Divine builder of Saqqara, right now your temple is being violated by the schemes of Memphis priests. Pharaoh's life is in danger!
Suddenly, the ibis-man seemed to tremble with anger.
By the gods! This can't be!
THE VENGEANCE OF THE IBIS WILL FILL THEM WITH FEAR!
And straight away, from the back of the tomb of a million ibises, a low rumbling shook the earth.
Such was the sound of the master's call, from the far reaches of the ages, that the ibises broke free from their imprisoning pots...
35

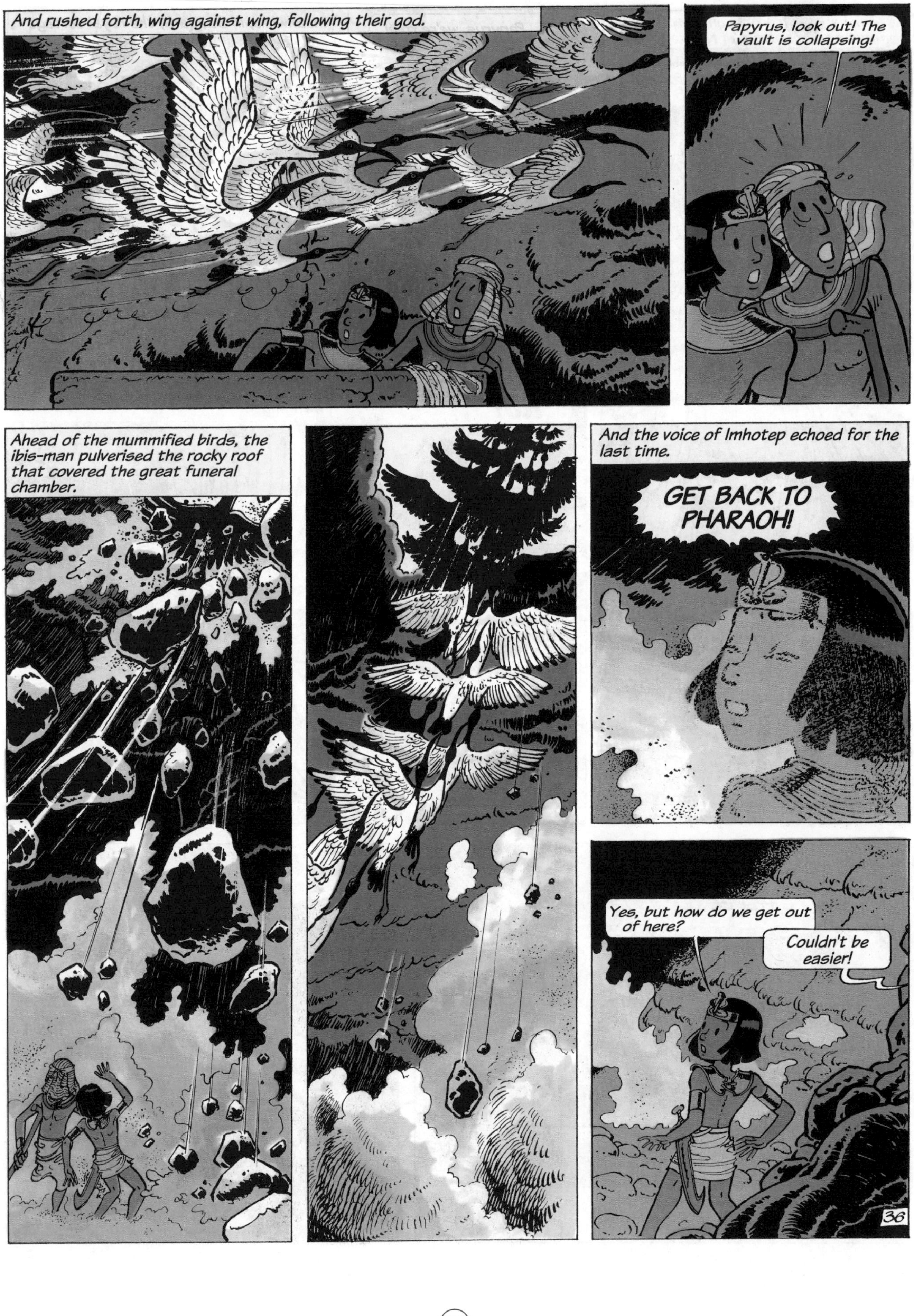
And rushed forth, wing against wing, following their god.
Papyrus, look out! The vault is collapsing!
Ahead of the mummified birds, the ibis-man pulverised the rocky roof that covered the great funeral chamber.
And the voice of Imhotep echoed for the last time.
GET BACK TO PHARAOH!
Yes, but how do we get out of here?
Couldn't be easier!
36

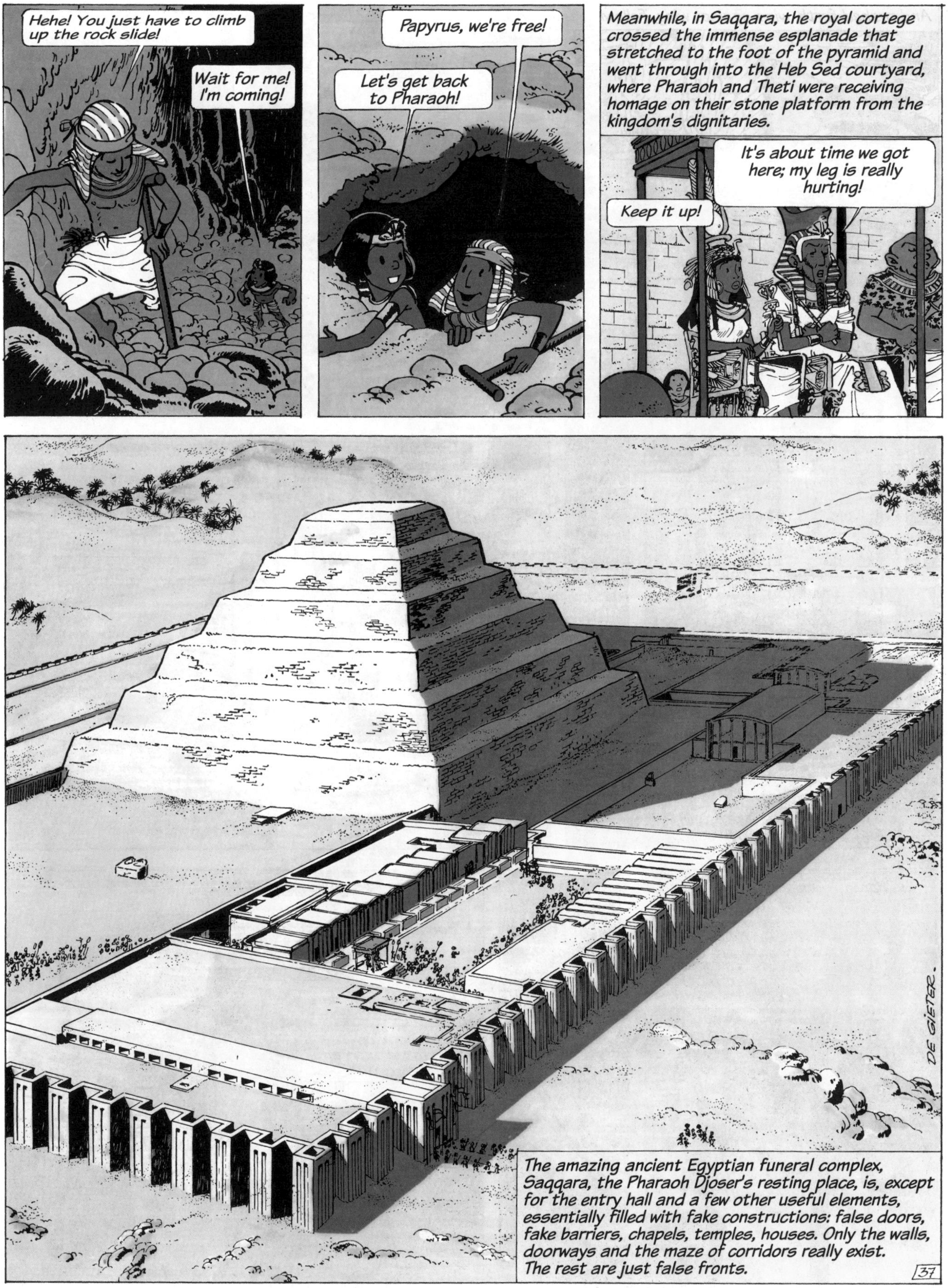

Hehe! You just have to climb up the rock slide!
Wait for me! I'm coming!
Papyrus, we're free!
Let's get back to Pharaoh!
Meanwhile, in Saqqara, the royal cortege crossed the immense esplanade that stretched to the foot of the pyramid and went through into the Heb Sed courtyard, where Pharaoh and Theti were receiving homage on their stone platform from the kingdom's dignitaries.
Keep it up!
It's about time we got here; my leg is really hurting!
DE GIETER.
The amazing ancient Egyptian funeral complex, Saqqara, the Pharaoh Djoser's resting place, is, except for the entry hall and a few other useful elements, essentially filled with fake constructions: false doors, fake barriers, chapels, temples, houses. Only the walls, doorways and the maze of corridors really exist. The rest are just false fronts.
37

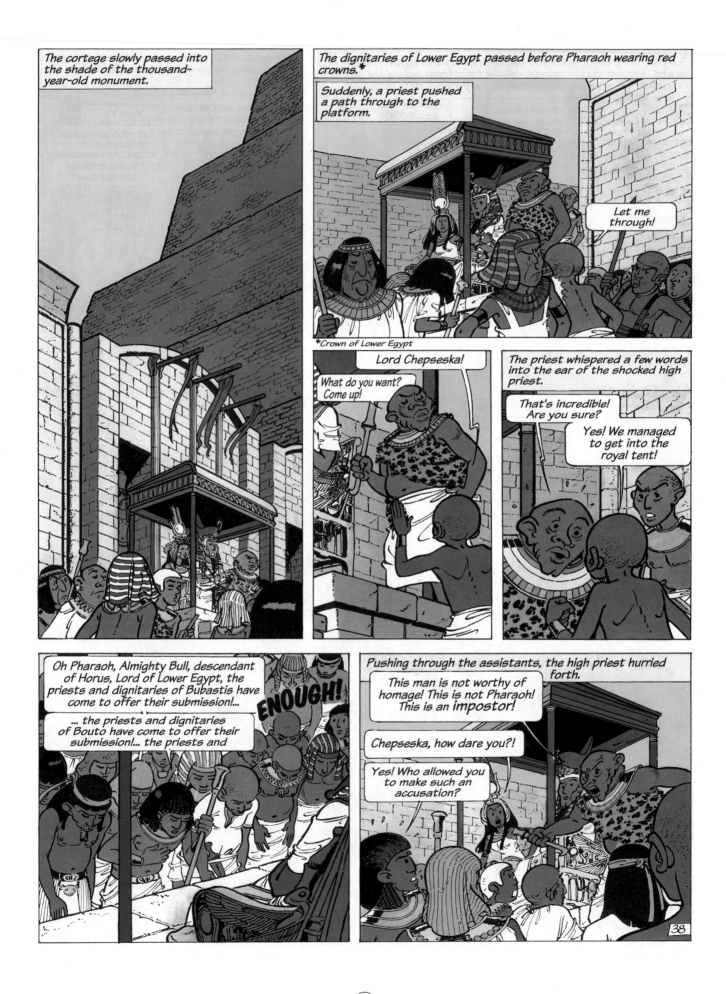

The cortege slowly passed into the shade of the thousand-year-old monument.

The dignitaries of Lower Egypt passed before Pharaoh wearing red crowns.*

Suddenly, a priest pushed a path through to the platform.

Let me through!

*Crown of Lower Egypt

Lord Chepseska!

What do you want? Come up!

The priest whispered a few words into the ear of the shocked high priest.

That's incredible! Are you sure?

Yes! We managed to get into the royal tent!

Oh Pharaoh, Almighty Bull, descendant of Horus, Lord of Lower Egypt, the priests and dignitaries of Bubastis have come to offer their submission!...

... the priests and dignitaries of Bouto have come to offer their submission!... the priests and

ENOUGH!

Pushing through the assistants, the high priest hurried forth.

This man is not worthy of homage! This is not Pharaoh! This is an impostor!

Chepseska, how dare you?!

Yes! Who allowed you to make such an accusation?

38

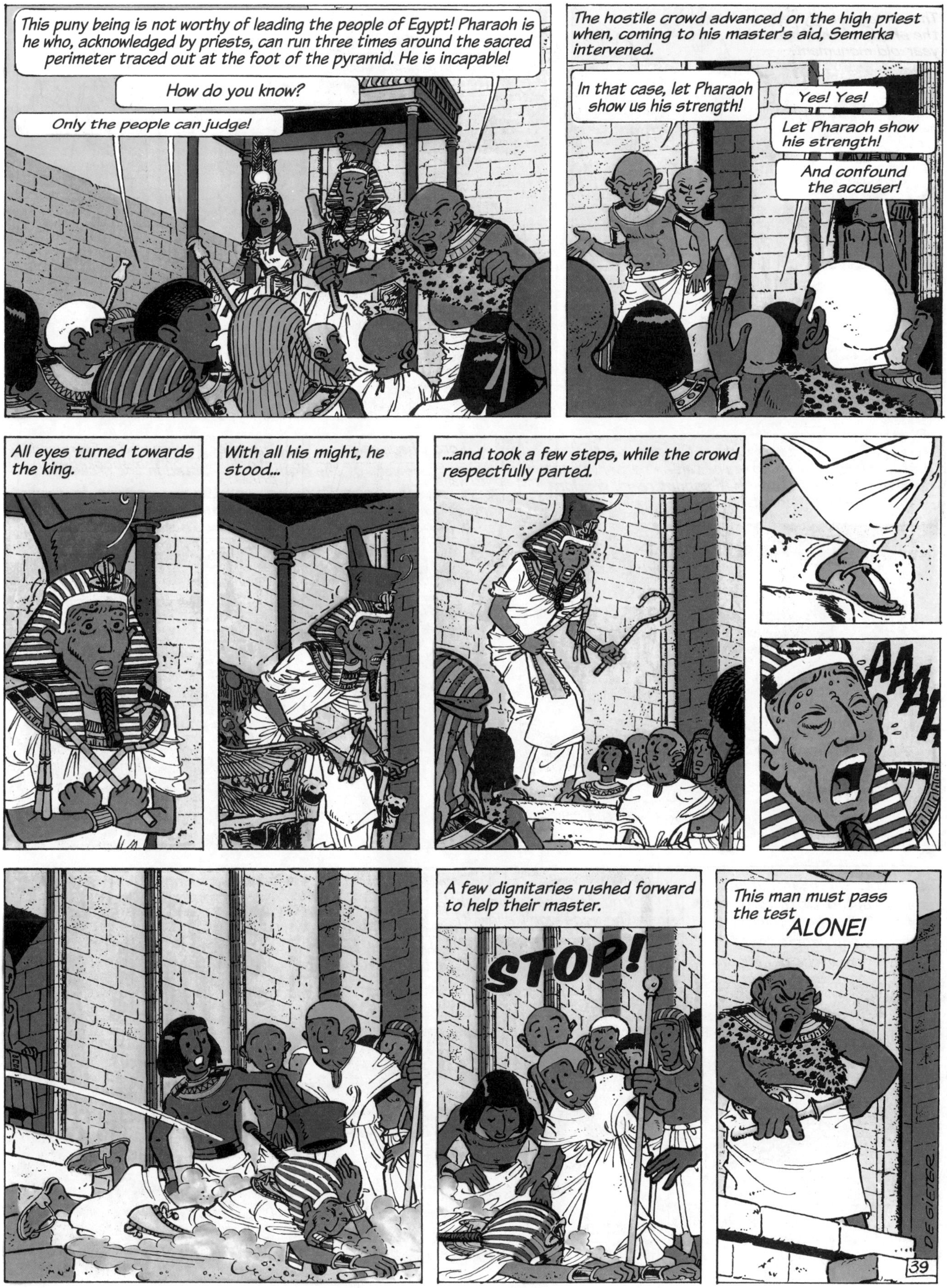
This puny being is not worthy of leading the people of Egypt! Pharaoh is he who, acknowledged by priests, can run three times around the sacred perimeter traced out at the foot of the pyramid. He is incapable!
How do you know?
Only the people can judge!
The hostile crowd advanced on the high priest when, coming to his master's aid, Semerka intervened.
In that case, let Pharaoh show us his strength!
Yes! Yes!
Let Pharaoh show his strength!
And confound the accuser!
All eyes turned towards the king.
With all his might, he stood...
...and took a few steps, while the crowd respectfully parted.
AAAA
A few dignitaries rushed forward to help their master.
STOP!
This man must pass the test ALONE!
DE GIETER
39

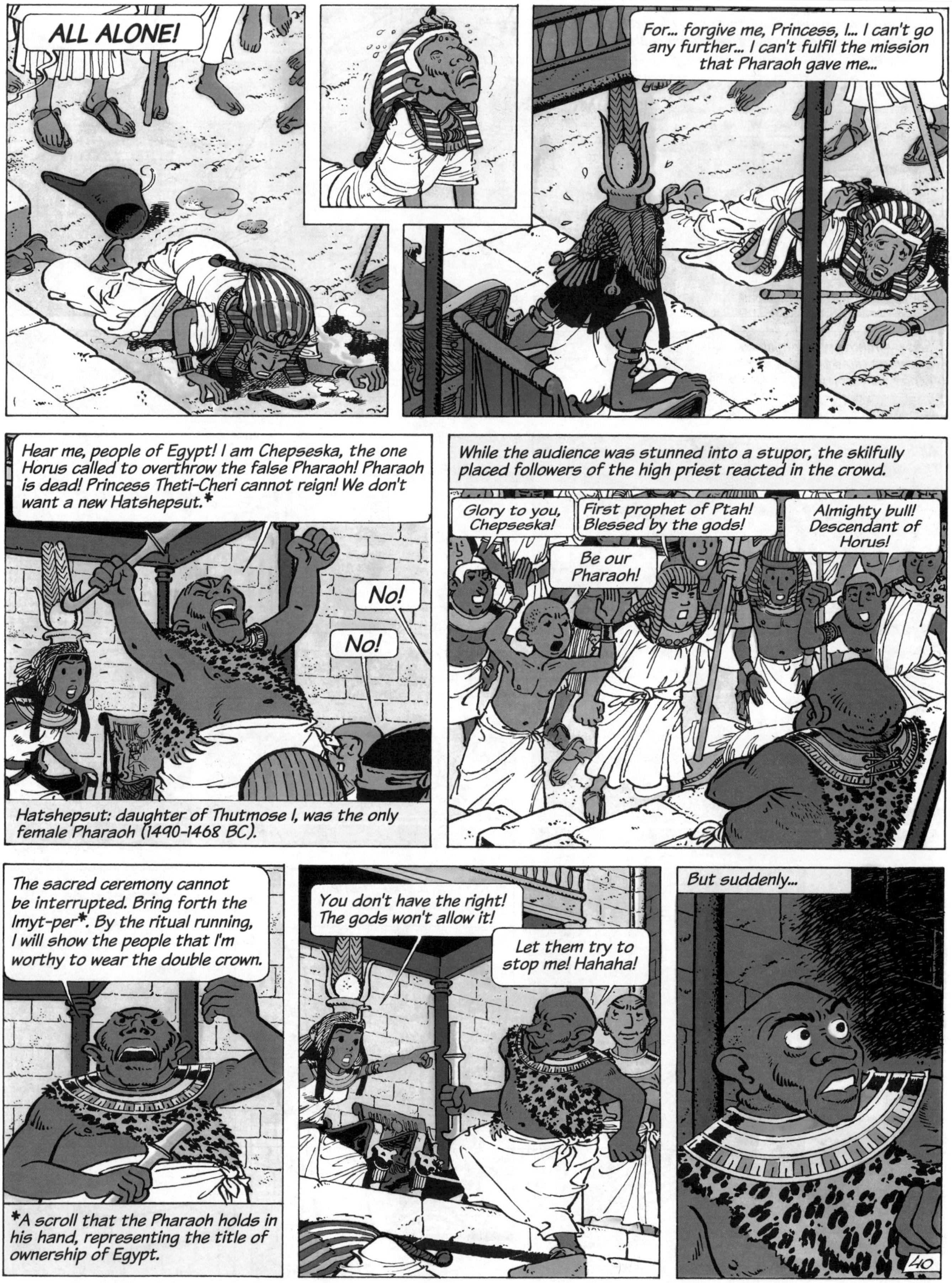
ALL ALONE!
For... forgive me, Princess, I... I can't go any further... I can't fulfil the mission that Pharaoh gave me...
Hear me, people of Egypt! I am Chepseska, the one Horus called to overthrow the false Pharaoh! Pharaoh is dead! Princess Theti-Cheri cannot reign! We don't want a new Hatshepsut.*
No!
No!
Hatshepsut: daughter of Thutmose I, was the only female Pharaoh (1490-1468 BC).
While the audience was stunned into a stupor, the skilfully placed followers of the high priest reacted in the crowd.
Glory to you, Chepseska!
First prophet of Ptah! Blessed by the gods!
Almighty bull! Descendant of Horus!
Be our Pharaoh!
The sacred ceremony cannot be interrupted. Bring forth the Imyt-per*. By the ritual running, I will show the people that I'm worthy to wear the double crown.
*A scroll that the Pharaoh holds in his hand, representing the title of ownership of Egypt.
You don't have the right! The gods won't allow it!
Let them try to stop me! Hahaha!
But suddenly...
40

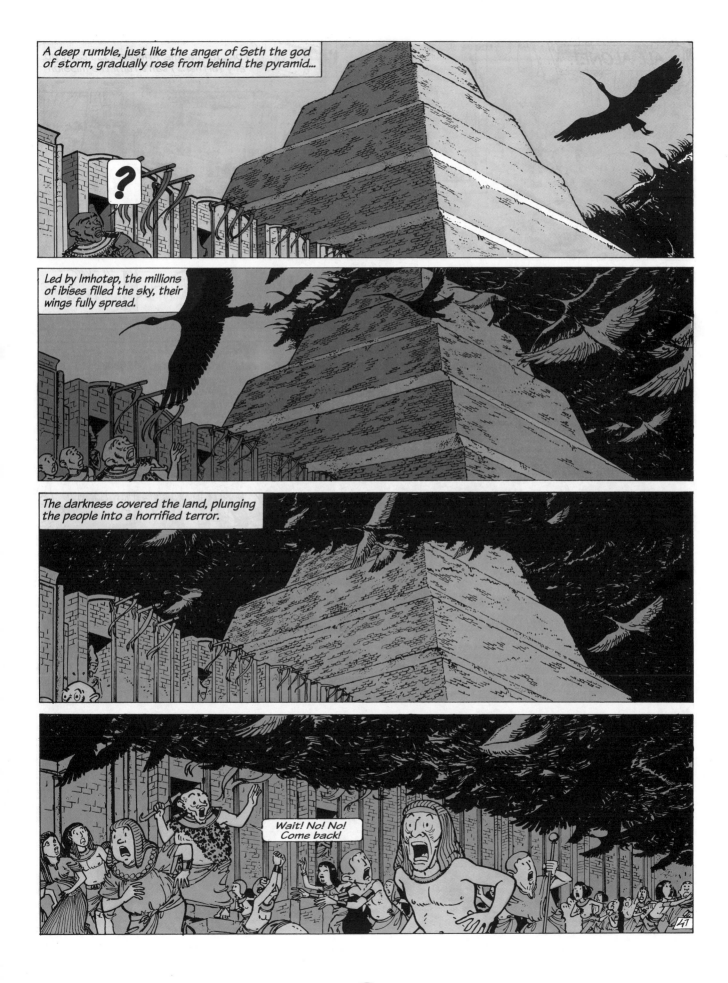

A deep rumble, just like the anger of Seth the god of storm, gradually rose from behind the pyramid...

Led by Imhotep, the millions of ibises filled the sky, their wings fully spread.

The darkness covered the land, plunging the people into a horrified terror.

Wait! No! No! Come back!

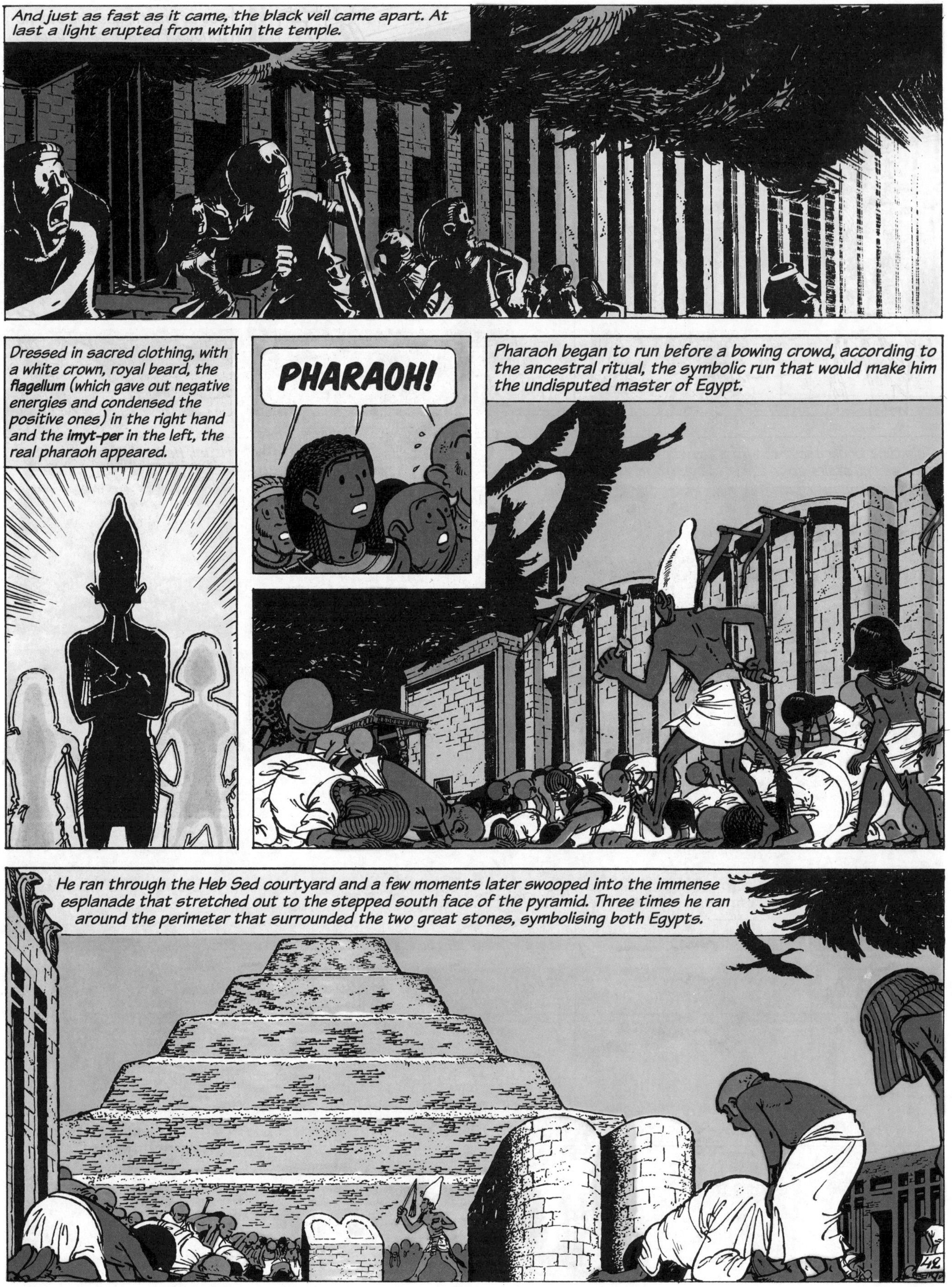
And just as fast as it came, the black veil came apart. At last a light erupted from within the temple.
Dressed in sacred clothing, with a white crown, royal beard, the flagellum (which gave out negative energies and condensed the positive ones) in the right hand and the imyt-per in the left, the real pharaoh appeared.
PHARAOH!
Pharaoh began to run before a bowing crowd, according to the ancestral ritual, the symbolic run that would make him the undisputed master of Egypt.
He ran through the Heb Sed courtyard and a few moments later swooped into the immense esplanade that stretched out to the stepped south face of the pyramid. Three times he ran around the perimeter that surrounded the two great stones, symbolising both Egypts.

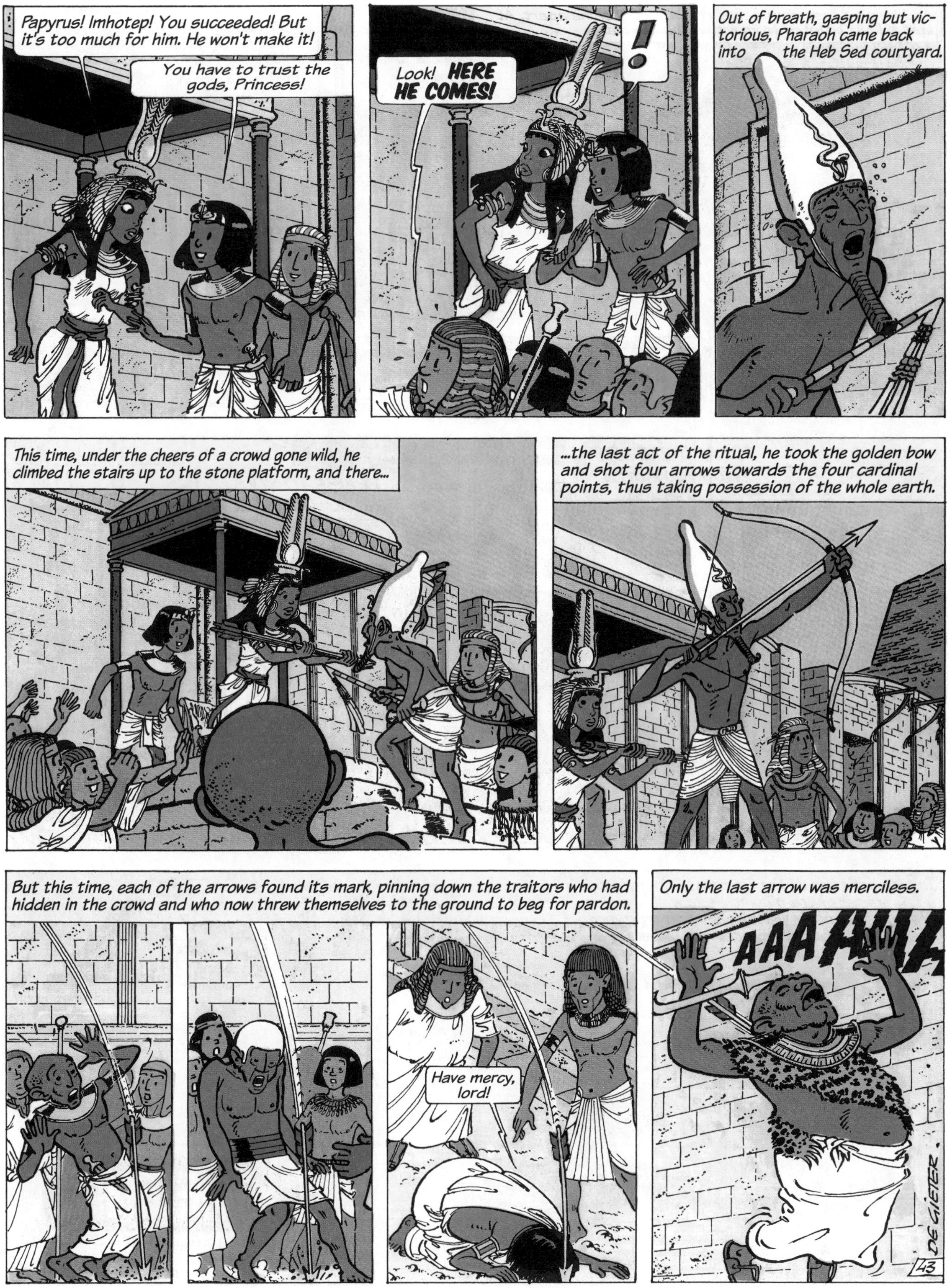
Papyrus! Imhotep! You succeeded! But it's too much for him. He won't make it!
You have to trust the gods, Princess!
Look! HERE HE COMES!
!
Out of breath, gasping but victorious, Pharaoh came back into the Heb Sed courtyard.
This time, under the cheers of a crowd gone wild, he climbed the stairs up to the stone platform, and there...
...the last act of the ritual, he took the golden bow and shot four arrows towards the four cardinal points, thus taking possession of the whole earth.
But this time, each of the arrows found its mark, pinning down the traitors who had hidden in the crowd and who now threw themselves to the ground to beg for pardon.
Have mercy, lord!
Only the last arrow was merciless.
AAAHHA
DE GIETER
43

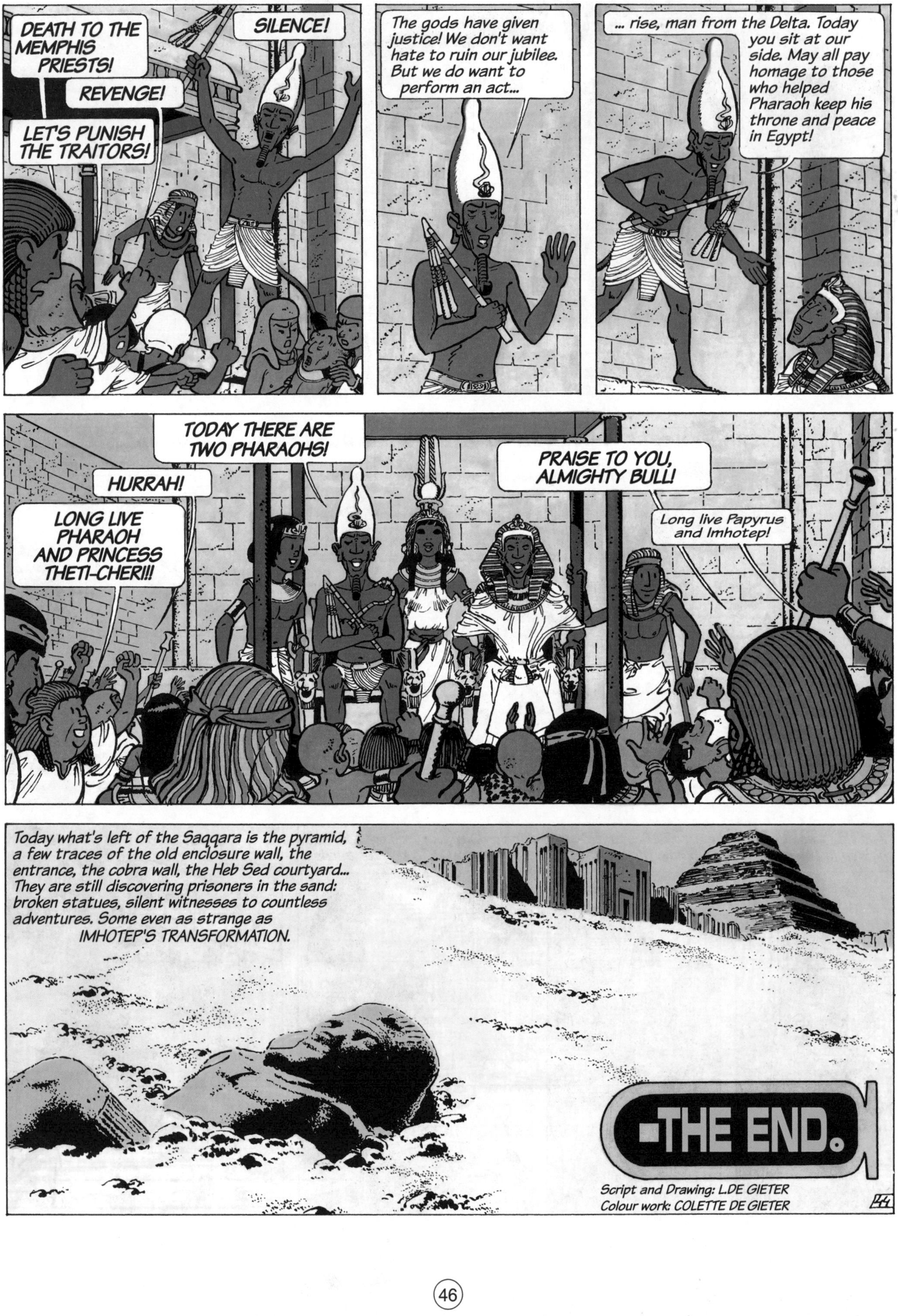
DEATH TO THE MEMPHIS PRIESTS!
SILENCE!
REVENGE!
LET'S PUNISH THE TRAITORS!
The gods have given justice! We don't want hate to ruin our jubilee. But we do want to perform an act...
... rise, man from the Delta. Today you sit at our side. May all pay homage to those who helped Pharaoh keep his throne and peace in Egypt!
TODAY THERE ARE TWO PHARAOHS!
HURRAH!
LONG LIVE PHARAOH AND PRINCESS THETI-CHERI!!
PRAISE TO YOU, ALMIGHTY BULL!
Long live Papyrus and Imhotep!
Today what's left of the Saqqara is the pyramid, a few traces of the old enclosure wall, the entrance, the cobra wall, the Heb Sed courtyard... They are still discovering prisoners in the sand: broken statues, silent witnesses to countless adventures. Some even as strange as IMHOTEP'S TRANSFORMATION.
THE END.
Script and Drawing: L.DE GIETER
Colour work: COLETTE DE GIETER

1 - THE RAMESES' REVENGE

2 - IMHOTEP'S TRANSFORMATION

COMING SOON

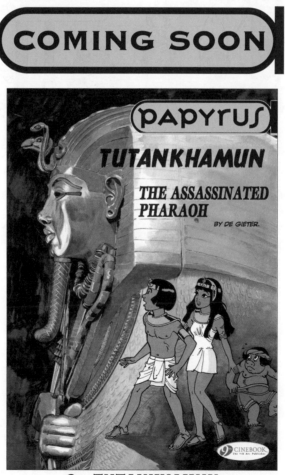

3 - TUTANKHAMUN
THE ASSASSINATED PHARAOH